GARDEN TREES

■ Step by Step to Growing Success ■

■ David Carr ■

CROWOOD GARDENING GUIDES

First published in 1988 by
The Crowood Press Ltd
Gipsy Lane
Swindon
Wiltshire SN2 6DQ

This paperback edition published 1991.

British Library Cataloguing in Publication Data

Carr, David *1930–*
  Garden trees. – Rev. ed.
  I. Gardens. Trees
  I. Title
  635.77

ISBN 1 85223 576 4

Picture Credits
Figs 2, 4, 11, 18, 44, 51, 52, 54, 60, 66, 72, 76, 77, 79, 80, 84, 86, 88 and 92
are courtesy of Dave Pike.
Figs 7, 12, 16, 17, 25, 27, 31, 33, 35, 46, 47, 67, 68, 69, 70, 73, 74, 75, 78, 81,
82, 85, 87, 93, 94, 95, 96, 97 and 98 are courtesy of Morris Nimmo.
Figs 1, 6, 7, 8, 61, 83 and 91 are courtesy of Natural Image.
Front and back jacket photographs courtesy of The Garden Picture Library.

All colour artwork by Claire Upsdale-Jones.

Typeset by Avonset, Midsomer Norton, Bath
Printed and bound by Times Publishing Group, Singapore

Contents

Introduction

It is strange, but a fact, that when standing in the midst of a mature landscape, well endowed with trees, the tendency is to take them completely for granted. It is only when confronted by the flat harshness of a new garden or housing development – invariably devoid of trees – that few fail to notice their absence and comment! Trees will add character, colour and interest to almost any garden setting, softening up hard architectural features and breaking up the skyline.

Healthy, properly managed trees, chosen to suit the site, are a real asset around any home. On the other hand, ill-chosen, badly sited, neglected trees are likely to be a distinct liability, and when trees become a nuisance, mistakes can very often be traced right back to planting time. Maybe the wrong variety was selected. Perhaps bad siting is to blame. Sometimes the fault lies in ignorance, sometimes in bad subsequent management. To ensure success with trees, some basic 'know-how' and understanding is required, and timely care and attention are called for as well.

Garden Trees is designed for anyone who wants to incorporate the beauty and majesty of trees into their own garden, however small the plot. It lays out the ground rules for good tree selection, planting, care and management, and highlights the surprising variety of trees which are now readily available. It aims to provide a launch pad for the gardener to develop a real interest

Fig I Acer japonicum 'Vitifolium' like other Japanese maples has outstanding autumn leaf tints – the colours are best on acid soils.

in the use of trees in garden design and layout, and will give inspiration for anyone who is planning a new garden, or who is revamping an existing one.

CHAPTER 1

Trees Around the Home

Trees are around for a very long time – and will certainly outlive those who plant them, and the two or three succeeding generations as well. Therefore it is important to give the matter of initial choice the consideration it deserves. A well-positioned tree can add considerable value to a home and can provide interest the year round.

When it comes to setting out trees in the garden, the design factors of scale and proportion need careful thought. Avoid creating any situation which smacks of the ridiculous. Trees should be of a size appropriate to the scale of the setting and be in proportion to other plants,

Fig 2 Laburnum – *a highly popular tree.*

buildings and features nearby. Do not, for example, plant a forest tree in a small modern garden. It looks wrong and in addition is bound to create some future nuisance. In time, not only will the garden be completely overshadowed, but the tree will need regular professional pruning if it is to be restrained and not overhang paths; nor rob light and air from the house; nor cause damage to foundations.

Garden trees catalogued as 'small' and 'medium' usually present few problems. They are a safe choice when buying the odd ornamental tree and are rarely out of keeping with their surroundings.

When using dwarf trees, place them in a setting which befits them. Plant them in a rock garden among low-growing alpines and heathers perhaps? And reserve miniature trees for such as a sink garden. Alternatively, use them in a bed with other plants of proportionate height. Never set them near tall shrubs or trees where they would be swamped.

Where trees are used near doorways and entrances, again the aim must be to keep them in scale with the setting. A cypress tree of 3½ft (1m) ultimate height may be fine on the patio, but a 7ft (2m) high specimen juniper would look better, say, near the front gate.

ABOUT TREES

Tree Shape

Trees come in many shapes and there is something to suit most tastes and situations. Many have a fairly distinct recognizable habit of growth and this should be exploited to best advantage.

Fig 3   Tree shapes: (a) Columnar; (b) Broad columnar; (c) Spreading;
(d) Single centre stem – weeping; (e) Conical;
(f) Rounded; (g) Domed; (h) Pendulous.

For instance, some varieties are naturally tall and narrow – columnar. They are likely to prove invaluable in confined spaces. Look out for Irish yew, Irish juniper, the Lombardy poplar cherry (*Prunus* 'Amanogawa') and the Incense cedar (*Calocedrus*). Weeping trees need more space, but make an excellent feature when grown as a single specimen. The most popular choices include *Cotoneaster hybridus* 'Pendulus', willow leaf pear (*Pyrus salicifolia* 'Pendula') and Kilmarnock willow (*Salix caprea* 'Pendula'). Most trees of globose or rounded habit are ideal for giving a contrast of shape in a small garden. Here plum leaf thorn (*Crataegus prunifolia*), Japanese cedar (*Cryptomeria japonica* 'Vilmoriniana') and *Thuja occidentalis* 'Danica' or 'Golden Globe' won't disappoint. Spreading deciduous trees are good on the eye, but they do need space. They are easy to fit into the less formal garden where planting of shrubs, herbaceous plants, ground cover and bulbs will flourish under their light canopy of shelter and shade. Cornelian cherry (*Cornus mas*), the great white cherry (*Prunus* 'Tai Haku'), Japanese crab apple (*Malus floribunda*) and winter flowering cherry (*Prunus* 'Autumnalis') rank with the best.

Planting schemes involving the use of different shapes by way of contrast need careful handling. Such arrangements can turn out well in experienced hands, but must not be overdone. This is a style of planting well suited to such as a rock garden, or bed, where dwarf trees of contrasting shapes are often used to good effect.

Deciduous and Evergreen

Regardless of their size and shape, trees are traditionally classified into two, sometimes three, categories, depending on their leaf dropping habits.

For practical purposes, deciduous trees shed their leaves in autumn. And in many cases leaf drop is preceded by brilliant autumn tints. In fact many of the most beautiful and colourful of garden trees are deciduous. And when it comes to trees able to withstand severe cold, along with the soot and grime of urban gardens, many are found among the deciduous varieties. They are tough. In small gardens leaflesss winter trees are not necessarily a drawback either. They rob less light from windows during the darker months of the year. Leaf dropping does, of course, create work and can present problems in the form of slippery paths and blocked drains and gutters. In situations where this nuisance is likely to be unacceptable, plant deciduous trees like birch or larch which are noted for their light leaf fall. Or choose evergreens. Evergreen trees, which retain their leaves throughout the year, are invaluable where winter interest and screening are a priority. But in any event, when assessing the overall garden situation, aim to have two evergreen trees/shrubs to each deciduous in an effort to fight excessive winter bareness. Generally speaking, evergreen trees are noted more for their foliage than for their flower and berry colour. Cotoneasters are outstanding exceptions.

Some trees are listed as semi-evergreen and can be relied on to retain most of their foliage in mild areas in average winters. However, they may drop their leaves under severe conditions.

GARDEN LAYOUT AND TREES

Traditionally, garden trees have had a fairly dominant role to play in creating a setting for the home. This was due, in part at least, to their ultimate size and height, which tended to dwarf most other plants into subservience. Today, with this in mind, it is still very important to take extra care when selecting and planting taller varieties to ensure they fit in with the overall plan. One well-placed, established tree will have a much greater impact in the garden in relation to an area of lawn, or beds and borders, taking up several times the equivalent space.

Garden Style

Undoubtedly, the whole question of choice of style is a matter of personal preference – a

Fig 4 Syringa *and* Prunus *make a good colour contrast.*

preference which is going to carry with it subsequent planting and maintenance implications. In theory, garden styles range from the highly formal, geometric approach at one extreme, to the near natural at the other. But in practice, most settle for a compromise somewhere in between.

In many small gardens, the more formal styles often prove the easiest to implement, especially if the garden is of the popular square or rectangular shape common in present-day housing development. In addition, if formal styles are based on the planting of a few wisely selected trees and shrubs, they represent a lot less work than an informal garden of herbaceous borders and filler plants offset with trees.

Whatever the style, consider tree habit very carefully and within the context of the full scheme. Those of a naturally neat habit make little work, whether in a formal or informal set-

ting. Most conifers are included here, along with the likes of flowering cherry, flowering plum, plum-leaved thorn and birch, which can be more or less left to their own devices. They need little more than the odd light thinning. On the other hand any attempt at topiary – the creation of geometric shapes for a formal setting – is very work intensive and will entail a regular commitment to pruning and clipping.

Siting for Decorative Effect

The correct positioning of trees is highly important in any style of layout, be it formal, informal or somewhere in between.

In a formal scheme, trees are frequently set out singly as a focal point, in a lawn or in a hard surfaced area, planted direct into the soil. This is perhaps the most common, most effective and

9

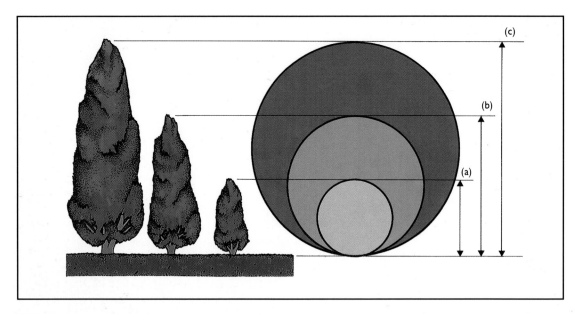

Fig 5   Tree growth.   Note the minimum root spread of an average tree in relation to height: (a) When young; (b) When half grown; (c) At maturity.

easiest way to use a tree. In a similar vein, a small tree can look equally effective when grown in a container and strategically placed on the patio or in a courtyard. Pairs of trees of identical shape and size look good framing doorways, drives and entrances, as they do when flanking tops or bottoms of flights of steps. Incidentally, it is the narrow columnar trees which are so well suited to and popularly used for this purpose. The embellishment of a dull corner with a tree, the tree-clad pergola-cum-tunnel and, where space permits, the tree-lined driveway all give a formal touch. And, although less frequently planted these days than in years gone by, some mention must be made of rows of pleached trees used to form clipped walls of green to create shaded walks. Limes are the trees most often chosen for this work. But again it is lack of space and demands made on labour which are the limiting factors in modern gardens when undertaking to grow trees in this way. For the most ambitious, one or more flowering crabs trained espalier fashion on to an archway, can make an unforgettable sight at flowering and fruiting time.

Wall-trained trees in the form of fans, espaliers and cordons are further manifestations of formality worthy of consideration, no matter whether for fruit or decorative use.

The scope for the informal planting of trees for effect is equally as varied as the formal. A single, wisely chosen specimen tree can, if suitably sited, be used informally. When the likes of magnolia, mountain ash or birch are set out to naturalize midst low-growing shrubs, herbaceous plants, or even in grass underplanted with bulbs, they soon become a garden-worthy feature and need little work.

Where space is available, a popular and most effective semi-formal approach is to plant a tree such as the Kilmarnock willow, or another eye-catching tree like the liquidambar, near water. When and wherever possible, seize the opportunity to capture the reflection of foliage, flowers and form in water for a pleasing effect of tranquillity.

Staying with the larger garden for a moment, groupings of three or five trees can look very distinctive as a focal point. But newcomers to the game are well advised to stick to varieties of one

TREE FORM – USES OF NATURAL SHAPES

Shape	Uses							
Conical	FP.	G.	P.	R.	SS.	L.	C.	ED.
Columnar	FP.	G.	P.	WS.	R.	SS.	L.	ED.
Broadly columnar	FP.	WS.	R.	L.	ED.			
Globose	FP.	G.	P.	R.	SS.	L.	C.	ED.
Spreading	FP.	WS.	L.					
Weeping-domed	FP.	P.	WS.	SS.	L.	C.	ED.	
Weeping-spindle	FP.	P.	WS.	SS.	L.	C.		
Weeping-pendulous	FP.	P.	WS.	L.				

Uses:	FP.	=	Focal point when planted singly
	G.	=	Grouped
	P.	=	Patio
	WS.	=	Waterside
	R.	=	Rock garden
	SS.	=	Small space
	L.	=	Lawn
	C.	=	Container
	ED.	=	Entrance or doorway

Fig 6 Picea pungens *'Glauca Pendula'* with its glaucous blue foliage looks well in the sun – as a companion to heathers of most colours.

family, say flowering cherries. However, with experience, or when offered sound advice, the contrasting of tree shape, flower and foliage interest within groupings becomes less risky. One of the best starting points is possibly conifers. Conifer groupings are extremely effective, and with container-grown stock there is the decided advantage of 'trial and error' experimentation with arrangements at the garden centre. It is not difficult to obtain a pretty fair idea of the overall final effect.

The random planting of dwarf and slow-growing trees, notably conifers, among heathers, to give height and contrast is as popular as it is labour saving, especially when planted on sloping ground which sweeps towards the viewer. Try them amongst other ground cover plants too. Yet another very satisfying form of planting is the island bed or border, devoted almost exclusively to dwarf and slow-growing tiny trees in a casual or informal arrangement.

Colour Interest

Colour is found not only in flowers, but also in bark, foliage and fruits. This may be stating the obvious perhaps but invariably these features are not considered. There is a distinct lack of awareness of the full potential.

When planning any layout involving the use of trees, keep in mind the changes in and duration of colour which accompany each season. Some spring blossoms last only a week at most – peach and almond blossoms are over in only a few days, less if it rains or the wind gets up. Some autumn tints last but a fortnight – cherry is over very quickly. It is what happens in between to maintain interest which usually swings the balance and settles the choice of tree for most.

Flower colour alone may change quite dramatically from the tight bud stage to opening and then on to the fully expanded flower. Japanese crab, for instance, goes from very deep pink in bud, opening to pale pink, then turns white. Foliage colours also undergo various changes as the season advances. Deciduous trees like Japanese maples are valued for their autumn tints, but many varieties also produce note-worthy spring and summer leaf colour. The dif-fering light levels experienced throughout the day, and from season to season, will make pro-found changes to colour. Don't ignore the effects of strong sunlight and shade either.

As a general rule, when viewing the garden as a whole, simple colour schemes, involving only a few carefully chosen shades, are likely to be more successful than a mass of mixed colours. The brightest and strongest colours are the so-called basic or primary colours – red, blue and yellow. The most vivid and striking colour schemes are obtained by contrasting two basic colours, perhaps red with yellow or blue with yellow. Quieter effects are possible by harmonizing shades of the same colour: pinks with reds; yellows with creams; silvers with greys; and blends of greens. The scope for the latter is well il-lustrated by the immense variation in conifer col-ourings alone – from dark green through light to gold; from blue-green through glaucous to grey.

Fig 7 A mature Acer palmatum, *when in its autumn colours as here, it has few rivals for sheer brilliance of foliage.*

When selecting trees for maximum colour effect, it is important to consider walls, fences and background colouring as well as that of nearby plants. Where backgrounds are dark or in partial shade, opt for trees with light-coloured foliage and flowers. White and yellow shades stand out well. This is especially important where any tree is to be illuminated at night.

The oft quoted advice of placing light colours in front of dark is good and sound.

TREES IN PRACTICE

It is probably true to say that trees are planted in gardens more for cosmetic effect than for any other reason. Rarely is their full potential either considered or appreciated. In actual fact trees have much to offer. Some of the more obvious benefits now come under discussion.

Screening for Privacy

High on the list of priorities of most house-holders comes the desire for a bit of privacy and seclusion – in short, to avoid being overlooked by neighbours. One or two well-positioned trees can go a long way to relieving such irritations and so enhance the quality of life.

Where, for example, downstairs rooms, or the patio, are overlooked from high ground or upstairs windows nearby, a tree or trees may be planted so that the crown (branch framework) neatly blocks the line of vision. Varieties of cherry, plum, crab, thorn, whitebeam, rowan and willow, with their spreading or weeping habits are hard to beat for the purpose.

Shelter from Wind

In the average small garden there is only limited opportunity to use trees for shelter purposes. The norm is to restrict them and treat them as a hedge.

However, where space allows, trees will provide a first-class windbreak, provided they are

Fig 8 Magnolia kobus *makes a striking spring-flowered specimen tree. It needs shelter from cold winds when in bloom.*

wisely chosen and carefully sited. They should be reserved for the exposed boundary. Also, do steer clear of large varieties; they take up too much light and space in most gardens. If wind-breaks are to be really effective, they need to form a continuous barrier across the line of the direction of the prevailing wind.

Tree height is one of the most important factors in determining the area of ground which is sheltered. On level land, confidently expect protection on the sheltered side for a distance equal to about seven times the height.

Dense conifers and evergreens make the best shelter belts in all but the most exposed gardens.

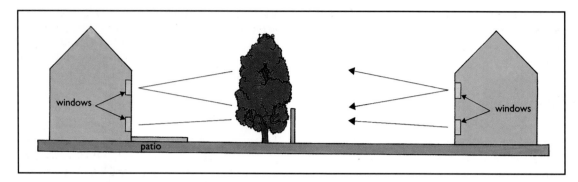

*Fig 9 Trees and amenity. The tree blocks out the neighbour's view on
to the patio as well as the downstairs and first-floor windows.*

But where protection is needed against intensely cold, freezing and drying easterly or northerly winds, opt for deciduous varieties. Many of these are hardier than evergreens and conifers. Provided they are pruned to create a bushy, filtering framework they will afford remarkable shelter.

Noise Reduction

The ability of garden trees and hedging to cut down on the noise levels from outside sources receives little recognition. It is an established fact, however, that where gardens and homes are situated near to noise centres like roads, railways, airports, football grounds, schools and play-grounds, trees will help to make life more tolerable.

Opt for those with a fairly dense texture. Conifers are ideal. Sparsely branched trees like laburnum are much less effective, but even these are better than nothing. Within limits, the taller the trees/hedging the greater the noise reduction.

Trees for Shade

Dappled shade under the canopy of trees is most welcome in locations of high light intensity and strong sun. Admittedly this is not a serious problem in many parts of the UK! However, in sunny, southern areas – especially near the coast – the glare from highly reflective surfaces, windows, conservatories, greenhouses, cars and light-coloured paving can be a problem. Even in the British climate there are many occasions when some shade is desirable to be able to sit out-doors in comfort at midday. To give midday shade, set any tree or tree grouping almost due south. Incidentally, when planting trees to shade sitting areas, take good care not to block out late afternoon and evening sun. After all, this is the most likely time of day for these areas to be used.

There are many low-growing garden-worthy herbaceous perennials, shrubs, annuals, ground cover and bulbs which benefit from, and flourish under, the dappled shade of trees. Birch, coton-easter, laburnum, crab, flowering cherry and plum as well as robinia, rowan and whitebeam are among the trees most widely used for the purpose.

When and wherever it comes to planting trees to provide shade, give the matter plenty of thought. Take into account dull weather and the winter period when excessive shade could become a problem. Where there is a real danger of trees casting too much shade, then deciduous varieties offer certain advantages over ever-greens. Being leafless in winter, at a time when sunlight is scarce, they allow more light to reach plants at ground level. By a similar token, deciduous trees will not darken nearby windows to the same extent as evergreens.

Always be mindful that, other things being

equal, any garden planted up with trees will become increasingly shaded as time passes and the trees grow and flourish. So don't overdo things initially.

Temperature and Humidity

Exposure to wind and sun exerts a considerable influence upon the garden environment.

Tree plantings to give protection from wind keeps the garden a few degrees warmer than if fully exposed.

Tree shade keeps the garden a few degrees cooler during the day. However, at night it is a different story. An overhead canopy of leaves can afford a considerable degree of protection from frost on clear nights. This can make all the difference between success and failure where early spring-flowering camellias, magnolias and rhododendrons are grown.

Yet another effect of shelter from wind and protection from the full effects of hot, drying sun, is an increase in humidity. This is likely to alter the micro-climate under trees and in the garden in favour of plants such as ferns as well as foliage and flowering plants like hostas, rhododendrons and bleeding heart. Be wary, though, for excessive shelter, stagnant air and shade will encourage certain lawn diseases. In this event, some thinning out of branches will avoid serious troubles.

Soil Stabilization

Where new gardens are laid out on sloping ground, the planting of trees and shrubs can help to reduce erosion and stabilize the soil. But don't attempt planting on gradients of more than 1 in 2½ – these are better terraced. Obviously in small gardens, only dwarf or small trees can be of much help. Cotoneaster, holly, smoke tree and thorn are amongst the best.

Trees and Legal Responsibilities

The owner of a tree is held responsible for any damage it causes – whether to neighbours' property or to passers-by on the public highway or walking on public footpaths. Encroaching roots, and falling or overhanging branches are among the most common potential hazards.

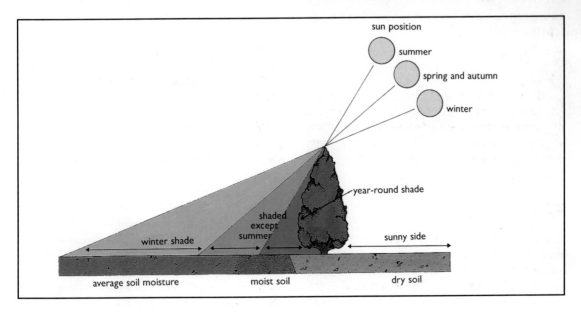

Fig 10   Trees, shade and moisture.

Be wary when planting near canals and water courses – there may be restrictions. Check with your local planning office.

Similarly, be cautious about planting near public utilities – power and water supplies. Again, check with your local planning office.

Never plant poisonous trees like yew where they can be reached by grazing animals.

THE TREE SCENE THROUGH THE SEASONS

The 'tree scene' as discussed in Chapters 2–5 is mainly about tree care in the form of a 'Calendar

Fig II Japanese Maples, such as this young Acer japonicum 'Aureum' are outstanding for their summer foliage.

of Operations'. Jobs which need to be tackled if trees are to flourish are pin-pointed to provide a useful basis for the guidance of readers.

If trees are to give of their best, it is important not only to attend to their needs in a proper manner, but at the correct time. And when deciding which jobs to do and when, and the order in which to carry them out, it is as well to keep the following points in mind.

Treework comes in two main categories. First, there are the urgent jobs demanding immediate attention if dire consequences are to be avoided, no matter the time of year. And here safety must head the list of priorities – where people or property are at risk, or the life of the tree is endangered. Trees which are rendered unsafe by storm or accident are the more obvious hazards. But the effects of disease and neglect on trees should not be underestimated either. Many such trees are very often in just as much need of emergency treatment if total loss is to be avoided, as indeed are those which are growing in containers and have inadvertently been allowed to dry out.

The remainder of treework falls conveniently in with the changing seasons. The best time to do the work depends on the nature of the work and individual circumstances. Within limits, do be flexible. Calendar dates can give a useful guide, provided due consideration is given to the prevailing conditions. There is not much sense in trying to plant trees, for example, if the weather and the state of the soil are quite unsuitable, no matter the calendar date. It is important that allowances are also made in order to take into account the slight variances from one region to another.

With many jobs there are 'ideal' times to do the work; and there are 'suitable' but 'less-than-ideal' times. What is the significance of this in practice? For one reason or another, it may not always be possible to undertake work at the 'ideal' time. A 'suitable' alternative cuts out the need to wait twelve months. In the calendars which follow, indications of ideal and suitable times are given.

CHAPTER 2

Summer – June to August

Any discussion about summer jobs would be incomplete without some reference to the likely weather, and its effect.

On fine days, the sun is at its most intensive. It is during these weeks of high temperatures, strong sunlight and long days of early summer, that trees in full leaf make maximum growth. Heavy demands are made on soil for moisture, at the very time of year when moisture loss normally exceeds rainfall. With healthy, deep-rooted, well-established trees, lack of surface moisture should not pose a serious threat. But shallow-rooted, newly planted trees will soon begin to suffer. Those set out in late spring, with little opportunity to make new roots, are most at risk. Any tree struggling under adverse growing conditions, or recovering from damage or disease, will soon come under stress too, as will container trees unless watered regularly.

Competition for nutrients – as well as moisture – is particularly fierce during summer; whether it be from weeds and grass or nearby trees, shrubs, plants and hedging. So, watering, feeding and weeding all need watching. Any disturbance of the roots, destined to upset nutrient and water uptake, is best avoided at this time of year. Don't, for instance, plant out trees or cultivate deeply over their root run. Pests and diseases thrive in days of ample food supplies and high temperatures. Aphids, caterpillars and red spiders are amongst the first pests to arrive. Diseases such as moulds and mildews often turn up towards late summer with the onset of shorter days and early morning dew. A routine spray programme is justified for trees carrying edible fruit crops, as it is for the likes of ornamental peach and almond which are vulnerable to

Fig 12 Davidia involucrata, the handkerchief tree, so called because of its unusual white handkerchief-like flowers in early summer, makes a rather distinctive specimen tree.

serious attacks of peach leaf curl and red spider mite. However, for the vast majority of garden trees, it is normal to hold back chemical sprays until problems arise. Many are naturally resistant to attack and rarely need any special treatment. Mountain ash and Kilmarnock willow are notable representatives of the 'trouble free'.

> **Key**
> Ideal time**
> Suitable time*
>
> Groundwork – these jobs are soil or root related
> Treework – these jobs are concerned with the tree above ground

GROUNDWORK

Routine General Care

Watering ** Container trees must be kept reasonably moist at all times. This can mean watering daily – even twice daily and more during very hot weather. Water containers slowly and apply sufficient; carry on until water trickles out at the base. If the compost has been permitted to dry out and shrink back from the sides of the container, more drastic measures are called

for. With large immovable containers the best way is to infill, by packing moist compost down the sides using a pointed stick. Smaller potted trees should be submerged in a bucket of water, but only until the bubbles stop rising. Then remove promptly.

Deep watering ** Where established trees have been prepared and undercut in readiness for an autumn move, make sure the rootball doesn't dry out in a drought. Spike the ground with a garden fork to assist water percolation.

Feeding ** On poor and impoverished soils, and on sandy soils, trees benefit from an occasional liquid feed of high potash fertilizer – particularly in areas of high rainfall. But do not apply the feed more than once a month. If the soil is very dry, water all trees thoroughly on the day prior to feeding. Apply in the region of 4 gallons per sq yd (20 litres per sq m) over the estimated root run. Trees in containers can be fed to advantage every fortnight. The rules for liquid feeding are the same as those for watering – carry on until it trickles out from the container base. Don't feed new trees within twenty-one days of planting. Give delicate roots a chance to become established, otherwise there is a risk of scorching.

Weeding ** Wherever practical, aim to maintain a minimum 12in (30cm) wide collar of weed-free soil around the trunks of all trees. Weeds and grasses, if allowed to grow unchecked, will not only compete for moisture and food, but may also encourage rotting of the trunk and defoliation of the lower branches. There is no better breeding ground for pests – weevils in particular.

Handweeding is safer than using chemical weedkillers. While the aim must be to get weeds out by the roots, take care not to disturb the tree roots more than is absolutely necessary. Be sure to dig out self-sown trees like ash and sycamore which spring up in the garden. In particular, however, attend to those at the foot of house walls before they get a hold.

Fig 13 Provision for deep watering. When planting, place one drainpipe on each side of the rootball and pack around with soil. Water is poured down each pipe for deep penetration.

Mulching ** Where mulching was missed in spring, go ahead now. It is important to water thoroughly before forking on the mulch. Keep an eye on mulches put down in spring. During summer they will probably need replenishing. The ideal is to maintain a generous layer some 2–3in (5–8cm) thick throughout the growing season.

Cultivations ** Where trees are planted in beds and borders, and the soil is not protected by a surface mulch, occasionally hoe or lightly cultivate whenever weed seedlings show or a thin crust develops over the soil. This will kill off seedling weeds, create a dust mulch, and help to conserve soil moisture. But take special care not to go too deep when working round surface-rooting trees like magnolia.

Grubbing out ** Summer is a good time to deal with any apparent tree casualties. But do examine valued trees for any sign of life before felling. One good, time honoured way, is to scrape away bark, on the newest wood, with the thumb nail. If any sign of green is exposed, give the tree the benefit of the doubt for another few months at least.

After felling, dead stumps can, if left, attract and become a host for the dreaded honey fungus disease. The fungus is then liable to go on to attack and kill other healthy shrubs and trees nearby. So old stumps need prompt attention. Ideally they are best dug out and burnt. Where stumps are too big or inaccessible another practical solution is to treat with chemical. Saw off the trunk as close to the ground as possible. Then drill a series of ½in (1cm) holes into the stump. Make the holes about 2in (5cm) deep and a similar distance apart – as near to the vertical as possible – working systematically over both top and sides. Half fill each hole with crystals of nitrate of potash and plug right away with cork or wooden dowel to keep out of the rain. Examine the holes regularly and top up as necessary – this is usually three or four times a year. The nitrate of potash will speed up the decomposition process. The larger the stump and the harder the wood, the

longer it takes, but given time all will eventually rot. Allow anything from about two to ten years. To camouflage while rotting down, plant around the stump with spreading shrubs or ground cover.

Care of New Trees – Extra Work

Watering ** Keep newly planted trees well watered. This is vital during their first summer. During dry weather apply at least 2 gallons (10 litres) per tree every three or four days. Soak the rootball thoroughly rather than watering in dribbles which encourages undesirable surface rooting. The deeper the roots the better able are trees to withstand dry weather. Step up watering to daily or every other day during periods of prolonged drought and on light, sandy soils.

Deadheading ** Gently pick or cut off dead and faded flowers on young trees. This is to prevent seeding and fruiting. This advice applies equally to ornamental trees renowned for their colourful fruits and berries and to edible fruits. Trees should not be allowed to carry fruit during the first season after planting, otherwise there is a risk that small trees will outgrow their strength and suffer a setback.

Propagation ** Keep young, growing-on stock well fed, watered and weed-free. Control pests and diseases rigorously.

Shade and ventilate any young trees in frames. Give gradually increased air in the case of newly rooted cuttings.

Ground preparations ** and * Summer is a good time to clear out overgrown and neglected land, and to carry out all the necessary cultivations and weedkilling in time for autumn planting. By a similar token complete grading, levelling and drainage. See page 30.

Manure, cultivate and lime any ground intended for associated planting in the immediate vicinity of the proposed plantings of trees.

Prepare hard standing areas for container trees

19

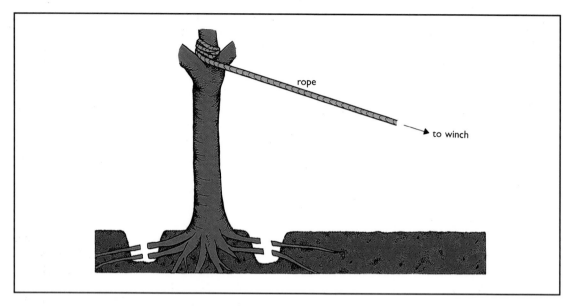

Fig 14 Tree stump removal: (a) Saw off the branches, leaving a good length of trunk to provide good leverage to pull on; (b) Attach a rope high up the tree and fasten the other end to a winch; (c) Dig around the tree and cut the main roots before winching out.

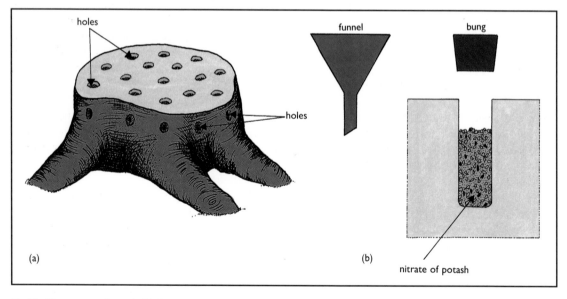

Fig 15 Tree stump disposal: (a) The stump is sawn off close to ground level. Holes are drilled into the wood and partly filled with nitrate of potash using a funnel. The holes are then each plugged with a bung. (b) An enlarged side view of a single hole containing nitrate of potash ready to be sealed with a bung.

Fig 16 Sorbus aria 'Lutescens' is attractive in summer, but is best seen when its red and gold autumn leaf tints are set off by scarlet berries.

as an extension of existing hard surfaced areas. Level off site, remove and stack topsoil, then spread a 3–4in (8–10cm) layer of gravel.

Firming in ** and * Refirm the soil around the roots of any newly planted trees, spreading fresh soil over any exposed roots and firming again.

Containers and composts ** and * Order up and bring to hand all containers and potting composts needed for autumn planting.

Sitework ** and * Build any walls and erect fences and terraces by way of protective shelter and screening for young trees. This is a good time, too, to construct any permanent features like pergolas, arbours and arches.

TREEWORK

Routine General Care

Tree supports ** Check tree supports and ties at least once every summer.

Removal of suckers ** Suckers are unwanted growths which usually arise at or below soil level on grafted trees. Either carefully pull each sucker away from, or cut back to, the point of origin – to avoid regrowth.

Pruning ** Summer prune wall-trained ornamental trees grown as cordon, fan or espalier. But wait until the new season's growths have made at least five to nine leaves. In practice this normally means starting to prune in early to late June, depending on site and soil, and continuing through into August. Similarly, prune other intensive trained tree forms.

Prune ornamental cherries, plums and peaches during July and August to minimize the risk of silver leaf infection; the wounds self-heal naturally during summer.

Selectively thin out branches, to relieve the strain on trees previously undercut and prepared for an autumn move.

Sanitation pruning – the removal of dead, badly diseased or seriously pest-infected branches – should be undertaken as and when necessary, regardless of the time of year. On old or neglected or overcrowded trees, thin out branches to let in light and improve air circulation. Push ahead with lopping and limited crown raising of old/neglected broad-leaved evergreens and conifers. Hold back on deciduous kinds until they have dropped their leaves in autumn.

Remove frost-scorched or browned foliage from conifers, the legacy of a hard winter, cutting cleanly back. See Chapter 6.

Bark tracery ** Doctor up any damaged or badly diseased bark by cutting out and paring over with a sharp knife. Paint over any wounds so exposed immediately with a safe proprietary fungicidal sealing preparation.

Propagation ** Take semi-ripe cuttings of cotoneaster, dogwood, stag's horn sumach, strawberry tree, tamarisk and willow. Root in a propagator, cold frame or on a cool indoor windowsill, shaded from midday sun.

21

Bud the following: apple (including crab), birch, cherry, holly, maple, peach, pear, plum, rowan, thorn and whitebeam.

Pest and disease control ** Keep a watchful eye for any serious outbreaks and take prompt measures at the first signs of trouble.

Care of New Trees – Extra Work

Watering ** Gently hose clean water over the foliage of new trees. Do this in the evening, following dry warm days or a buffeting by drying winds to reduce the stress and freshen them up.

Fig 17 Robinia pseudoacacia 'Frisia' retains its soft fresh greeny-gold foliage colouring all summer – turning golden before leaf drop in autumn.

Shading ** Continue to provide temporary shading for newly planted trees during hot spells. Fine mesh netting or lath screens supported on a light frame will suffice. Similar shading is particularly important for container plants during summer.

Tying in ** With wall-trained and formal trees, make sure new growths are tied in promptly if wind damage and breakages are to be avoided.

NEW TREES – PRE-PLANTING CONSIDERATIONS

Many trees take a long time to grow, develop and reach maturity. So it may be years before errors made at planting time become apparent. But when they do, and the realization sets in that things are disappointingly wrong, corrective steps will often prove expensive or unsatisfactory, and they are always wasteful of time and effort.

So to be reasonably certain of success, take stock of the site, soil and climate. Only when fully armed with this knowledge, set about deciding on a tree which is preferably in harmony with, or at least has a sporting chance of tolerating, the prevailing conditions. In short, first match the tree to the site, and then consider design factors like shading, screening and appearance.

ASSESSING THE SITE

Climate and Temperature

The climate, with special reference to temperature, is one of the most powerful influences likely to affect tree growth and survival. For practical purposes, the British Isles can be broadly divided into three main climatic regions – cold, average and mild.

Gardens in the cold climate areas of northern England and Scotland have long, hard winters with severe frosts and heavy snowfalls. Autumn comes early with frosts in September. Spring is late. Only the hardiest of garden trees can be relied on to have a reasonable chance of survival and give a good display of interest in due season.

The mild climate regions of much of southern England, the south coast and western seaboard districts permit the greatest choice of trees. Many tender varieties will even survive winter outdoors. The winters are relatively mild and the greatest number of frost-free days are enjoyed.

The average climate areas, which include much of central England, are intermediate in character between the extremes of the cold climate areas of the north and the mild southern and western districts.

The trees listed in Chapter 9 are given hardiness ratings which correspond to the regions where they can reliably be expected to survive the winter.

Rainfall Lack of rain should not present any problems when growing trees in the British Isles. All areas have a sufficiently high rainfall to support trees once they are established. However, western areas tend to be wetter than eastern and they are ideal for growing conifers.

Coastal areas In general, gardens near the coast, or other large expanses of water such as lakes and reservoirs, suffer less extremes of heat and cold. In winter the temperatures tend to remain a few degrees warmer, but in summer the water will exert a cooling effect. Extremely hot weather is unlikely.

Frost pockets Completely enclosed gardens, surrounded by high walls or fences, are a likely hazard when it comes to frost, even though sheltered from chilling winds. On clear, calm nights in spring, cold air collects at ground level and accumulates, rather like water in a pool. Similarly, gardens situated in hollows and valley bottoms are liable to collect cold air draining from higher ground, and are also at risk. In all these situations it is best to avoid planting early flowering ornamentals like camellia, magnolia and some of the flowering cherries and almonds.

South- and west-facing walls have a warming effect. They behave rather like storage heaters. Sun heat, taken in during daytime, is given off at night. This helps to keep wall-trained trees a few degrees warmer, and gives valuable added frost protection in spring.

Light

Sunlight provides vital energy that plants need for normal growth and development.

When assessing the site, it is important to bear in mind that sunlight and shade exert a powerful influence on trees – an influence which is inter-related with all other garden plants.

Before planting, note down which parts of the garden receive full sun for all or most of the day. Note, too, the seasonal variations between mid-summer when shadows are shortest, and mid-winter as they lengthen. Note those areas which are partially shaded, as well as those in full or permanent shade. It will soon become evident that most gardens are a patchwork of light levels. These need to be considered from two main viewpoints.

First the context of how light and shade are liable to affect the trees themselves must be looked at.

Open, south-facing aspects, which are not overshadowed by nearby buildings and the like, normally provide the sunniest sites where most flowering and fruiting trees will flourish.

East-facing sites, backed by a wall, building, hedge or trees are shaded for part of the day. These sites are open to early morning sun and are treacherous to trees which are in leaf or flower in winter or spring. Morning sun after overnight frost invariably results in blackening and injury to buds and foliage, caused by a too rapid thaw. Stick to late-flowering deciduous varieties like laburnum, thorn and cotoneaster in these situations.

West-facing sites are also partly shaded, but they are much kinder and are safe for almost any tree in fact.

North-facing aspects, and north-facing sloping ground are often in permanent shade. Such

Fig 18 Chamaecyparis pisifera 'Boulevard' has attractive silvery-blue foliage and grows best in partial shade on lime-free soil.

sunless situations are cold sites, suitable only for the hardiest of shade-tolerant trees like Lawson cypress and juniper.

In many modern gardens, hemmed in by walls, fences and hedges, the lower levels are very often in partial shade, up to a height of about 7ft (2m) or so. This is not as bad as it seems. Most young trees are quite happy in these conditions. Above the 7ft (2m) mark, trees may well receive almost full sun – an ideal situation for mature trees.

As a rule-of-thumb guide, deciduous broad-leaved flowering trees are light-demanding. They need sun. Evergreens will tolerate partial shade or light, dappled shade. Exceptions to the rule are most pines, which shed their needles in shade, and those conifers and broadleaved evergreens with gold, silver, blue and variegated foliage – these need more sun if they are to colour well.

A second and very important consideration for the other occupants of the garden, is the amount of shade the trees are likely to create. As trees grow, so the garden becomes increasingly shaded. With this in mind, it is important not to opt for large-spreading varieties in small gardens. Be wary, too, when planting tall conifers like Leyland cypress and Lawson cypress which will cast long shadows in winter.

Consider, too, the nature of the shade cast by trees. An overhead canopy from broadleaved trees like birch will produce a light, dappled shade – conditions which allow many plants to grow quite happily below their branches. However, a dense overhead cover from evergreens like yew and cedar is likely to shut out too much light for any worthwhile underplanting to flourish.

The Soil

Knowing what kind of soil makes up the bulk of your garden helps to ensure success with trees in a number of ways.

Most garden trees will grow satisfactorily in any average, reasonably fertile garden soil. It is when the soil is far from average that problems arise and trees begin to show their quite definite preferences.

By getting to know the soil, it is then possible to select varieties to suit, and subsequently to vary their treatment – so avoiding mistakes in cultivations, manuring and feeding.

Soil composition The composition of soil largely determines its characteristics and behaviour, and provides valuable clues as to its treatment.

With the risk of over-simplification, soils are made up of a mineral fraction, organic matter, soil air and soil water.

It is the mineral fraction and organic matter which exert the greatest influences on soil behaviour, nutrient content and acidity – so pin-pointing the type of soil. The mineral fraction consists of stones and gravel, various grades of sand, silt and clay – and sometimes chalk. Dead and decaying residues such as peat, manure and garden compost, plus soil fauna and flora, make up the organic matter. Soil air and soil water fill up the spaces in and around the mineral particles and organic matter.

Soil texture For practical garden purposes and treework, soils are invariably grouped into the following main types, based on texture: heavy or clay soils, medium loam soil, sandy light soil and peaty moss or fen soils. There are, of course, varying graduations between each broad type.

To give a rough working guide as to soil type, take a small handful of soil and moisten to the consistency of still paste. Rub between thumb and forefinger. Does it feel sticky and greasy without any trace of grittiness? Does it polish to a shine when rolled into a ball? Does it dry to a hard lump? If so, a high percentage of clay is likely. If the soil is a healthy, darkish brown, doesn't feel really sticky and will squeeze into a ball, then the indications are that it is an ideal loam. For further proof, try rolling the ball out into a strand 8in (20cm) or so in length; this should then just about bend round into a circle before breaking. Alternatively, drop the ball – a good loam will shatter on impact. Where the soil sample feels distinctly gritty, expect a high proportion of sand. And finally, if the soil is dark and spongy, try looking at it under a magnifying glass. Numerous root-like fibres would suggest peaty soil.

Heavy or clay soils: These soils drain slowly and water tends to stand around after heavy rain. They are sticky and difficult to work when wet. In fact, no attempt should ever be made to cultivate clay soils when wet. They dry out slowly in spring and are slow to warm up. When dry such soils set brick hard. A shrunken, cracked, baked surface is typical in summer.

Medium loam soils: Lucky are the owners of gardens overlying loam soils. They are close to the ideal as regards physical condition. All are good blends of sand and clay and range from sandy loams to clay loams. Easy to cultivate they are moisture and nutrient retentive.

Sandy light soils: Sandy soils are relatively easy to work, so the term 'light soils' has arisen. These soils normally drain fairly rapidly after heavy rain. Nutrients are soon washed away, hence their reputation as 'hungry soils'. Sandy soils are quick to dry out in fine weather to the detriment of plants.

Peaty, moss or fen soils: These soils are common to the fenland areas of eastern England and East Anglia, along with the mossland areas of Lancashire and Cheshire. Peaty and moss soils are usually dark in colour and spongy in texture. They are associated with moss and wet ground. Provided these soils are reasonably well drained, they present few problems.

Soil lime content The lime status of any soil has an important bearing upon the ability of many trees to grow and flourish. Trees such as beech, yew and box normally grow well in lime-rich soils. Others, notably Japanese maple, spruce and fir, dislike alkaline conditions common to limy soil. If grown in such soils yellowing is likely to result.

One useful indicator as to the presence of significant amounts of lime/chalk in the soil, is the type of plants which grow well in the garden, or in neighbouring gardens. An abundance of clematis, viburnums and plants such as thyme are indicative of lime in the soil. If suspicious, dig down to at least a spade deep, noting the colour of the subsoil. If the subsoil becomes progressively paler, or even whitish, with increasing depth, suspect large amounts of chalk and do a pH test.

Use one of the low-cost test kits. The instructions are easy to follow and the results are simply read off on a pH scale using a colour comparison chart. Another alternative is to use a pH meter which gives a direct dial reading. Whatever the method, a pH reading of 6.5 and less indicates acidity or low lime content. A pH of 6.5 to 7 is about neutral with sufficient lime for most trees. Above 7 indicates a high lime content.

Soil depth In order to provide good anchorage and to sustain growth, trees need a greater depth of good topsoil than most other garden plants. Reckon on most trees which grow to 15ft (4.5m) or more in height needing a minimum 18–24in (45–60cm) depth of good topsoil.

Test the soil depth by digging down and taking note of three possible danger signals.

First, it is not uncommon for a shallow layer of good topsoil to overlie relatively infertile subsoil.

The subsoil should be dug out and replaced with good topsoil prior to planting.

Second, difficulties may be created by soil 'pans' in the top 2ft (60cm) or so of soil – drainage is impaired and roots are unable to penetrate. Panning may be due simply to a hard layer of compacted soil. This needs to be thoroughly broken up and loosened before planting. Another and more serious form of panning is due to the build-up of a hard layer of chemicals. A crowbar is usually needed to break up chemical pans – they are extremely hard and often flint-like. Vast amounts of garden compost, peat or manure should be worked into the ground, prior to planting, to help prevent a recurrence of the problem.

Third, a similar situation to panning can arise where a thin layer of soil overlies a bed of rock. Given this situation, reconsider planting trees in the ground and seriously think about trees in containers.

Subsoil drainage Poor subsoil drainage is another factor which, like panning, will seriously limit the depth of root run. Where water cannot escape to lower levels, it has no alternative but to accumulate after every downpour, reaching ever nearer the soil surface in wet weather. The depth of good topsoil is effectively reduced, while waterlogged roots drown and suffocate. If water lies on the surface for any significant length of time after rain has stopped, the soil obviously needs draining. Unfortunately, poor drainage is not always apparent from the surface. If in doubt, dig out a test hole during winter, in a low-lying position. Make it at least 18in (45cm) square and 12in (30cm) deep. Cover with such as the dustbin lid to keep out of the rain. Examine the hole at regular intervals and if standing water accumulates in the bottom to a depth of more than about 2in (5cm) set about draining the land. In the short term think about alternatives – grow in containers or construct raised beds.

SUMMER FOLIAGE

Broadleaved trees	
Acer palmatum and varieties	Japanese Maples
Betula pendula and varieties	Birch
Corylus maxima 'Purpurea'	Purple-leaf Filbert
Cytisus battandierii	Moroccan Broom
Fagus sylvatica 'Purpurea Pendula'	Weeping Purple Beech
Gleditsia triacanthus 'Sunburst'	Honey Locust
Koelreuteria paniculata and varieties	Golden Rain Tree
Malus 'Profusion'	Purple-leaved Flowering Crab
Prunus 'Pissardii'	Purple-leaved Plum
Pyrus salicifolia 'Pendula'	Weeping Silver Pear
Rhus typhina	Stag's Horn Sumach
Robinia pseudoacacia 'Frisia'	Golden False Acacia
Salix caprea 'Kilmarnock'	Kilmarnock Willow
Sorbus aria and varieties	Whitebeam
Sorbus aucuparia	Mountain Ash
Conifer	
Gingko biloba	Maidenhair Tree

CHAPTER 3

Autumn – September
to November

When working with trees, be resigned to the fact that most jobs are influenced by prevailing weather conditions. This is particularly so in autumn.

During September, the days become noticeably shorter, the nights get cooler, and in cold districts early morning frosts threaten tender trees and those growing in containers. Expect the first of the autumn gales by about mid-month – a test for tree ties and supports. September invariably produces some fine, clear days which are perfect for pushing ahead with preparations for planting and, in fact, for planting some evergreens in northern areas.

As autumn progresses into October, rain, strong winds and cloud become increasingly prevalent. Fog is not uncommon. Frosts are more intense. In northern districts, autumn tints and leaf fall are already under way. Ground conditions deteriorate as the soil becomes saturated. Time is running out for autumn digging.

November follows a similar pattern to October. As the weather turns colder and more wintry expect frequent fogs and mists. Gales and a few hard frosts see off the majority of leaves from deciduous trees and in cold northern districts, snow is likely to fall on high ground. The soil is usually too wet to attempt much ground-work. Hold back until things improve or risk puddling and subsequent long-lasting problems.

GROUNDWORK

Aim to complete all treework before tackling end-of-season ground clearance and cultivations. Otherwise it will be necessary to walk over newly cultivated ground – with the consequential options of leaving an untidy finish? Or double working? It is often a good idea to deal with a convenient area of the garden at a time, systematically completing the treework and then finishing off the groundwork.

Routine General Care

Most of the jobs at this time of year are of a remedial nature – to correct or in anticipation of problems.

Land clean up ** Complete any cutting back of underplanting and ground cover to neaten, shape and restrain. Clear away weeds and grass from the base of tree trunks. Rake up and burn prunings along with seeding and perennial weeds, or cart them to the local tip. Compost healthy leaves.

Cultivations ** Fork lightly to relieve compacted soil.

Root pruning ** If ornamentals like flowering cherry and plum are reluctant to flower, then root pruning can help. This can start in November and continue into December. See page 66.

Undercutting ** Small established trees, which are to be lifted and transplanted, need to be prepared a year or two before the move to lessen the shock. Transplanting is tricky; there is

27

always a risk that the tree will not survive. Any tree planted during the past five years stands the best chance. Don't attempt to move deciduous trees over 12ft (3.6m) in height, or broadleaved evergreens and conifers over 7ft (2m); 3–4ft (90–120cm) is a better bet. The more fibrous-rooted trees like conifers and the strawberry tree usually move with least setback. Prepare the tree by digging out a circular trench some 18–24in (45–60cm) out from the trunk, less for small trees. Make it a spade deep and wide. Cut through any thick roots crossing the trench, but work round and gently replace fine fibrous ones with the minimum of disturbance. Stake and tie the tree. Water to settle and subsequently keep watered. In spring mulch generously. In the case of older trees, extend the preparations over a period of two years. Cut a semi-circular trench in the first year, backfilling as before. Complete the circle in the second year. Undercutting encourages the development of a more compact root system better able to withstand a move.

Lifting and transplanting **   Now is the time to move trees which were prepared a year or more ago. Prepare the new planting hole – at least 2in (5cm) deeper and twice as wide as the estimated size of the rootball. Fork up the bottom, working in plenty of well-rotted compost before topping over with planting mix. See page 39.

Remove the supporting stake from the prepared tree. Tie in the lower branches to stop them getting in the way and becoming damaged. Spray conifers with anti-wilt preparation. Then, working from alternate sides, gradually free and ease up the rootball and wrap in plastic sheet or netting. This is to reduce the risk of breaking the rootball during the move. After positioning in the prepared hole, stake and tie. Then pack around with planting mix, a little at a time, and firm well.

It is vital to keep the soil moist for at least two years after transplanting any tree, and to hose the foliage during warm dry weather to lessen the stress. Protect conifers and evergreens from wind. Mulch generously throughout the growing

Fig 19 Preparing a tree for lifting. Cut out a circular trench 18–24in (45–60cm) away from the base of the tree. Sever all thick roots as digging proceeds.

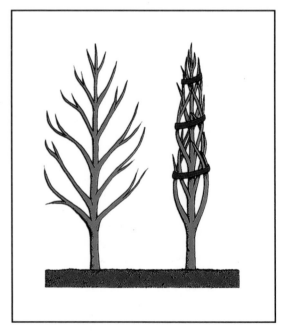

Fig 20 Moving trees – tie the branches of trees before lifting and transplanting.

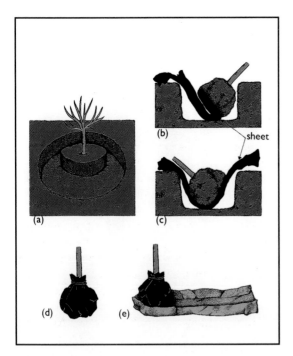

Fig 21 Lifting established trees: (a) Dig out soil to expose rootball; (b) Tilt rootball to one side and work a plastic sheet around and under; (c) Tilt rootball in reverse direction and pull plastic sheet from underneath; (d) Tie plastic sheet around the rootball. (e) Transplanting trees. Ease heavy rootballs on to a strong plastic sheet or old sack and drag along the ground gently to their new planting position.

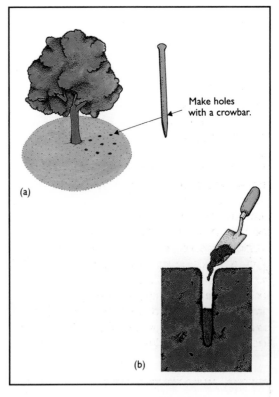

Fig 22 Feeding trees. (a) Feed old trees by making a series of holes about 12in (30cm) deep under the branches out to the extremities; (b) Fill each hole to the top with rich potting compost.

season, but don't feed until the roots have had a chance to get established. Give them about a year.

Feeding old trees ** This is of benefit in cases of obvious neglect or when there is a lack of vigour. One good way to get fertilizer, air and water down to the roots is by boring and topdressing. Bore holes up to 1½in (4cm) in diameter, making them 10in (25cm) deep and about 20in (50cm) apart. Work systematically over the entire root run. A soil auger is the ideal tool for the job, but most people make do with a crowbar. Fill each hole with a good soil-based potting compost like John Innes No 3. Brush it in and prod home with a pointed stick. Water in afterwards if dry.

Overturfing ** Associated with old trees in lawns, comes the problem of roots rising above ground. These not only make mowing difficult, but create a tripping hazard. The remedy is to lift the turf to expose the roots, cover over with up to 2in (5cm) of topsoil, grading the levels into the surrounding lawn before replacing the turf.

Changing ground levels ** When altering a garden layout, the soil level near existing trees may need to be adjusted.

When lowering levels around a tree, cut away soil and roots, but avoid cutting in closer to the tree than a distance equal to half that from the trunk to the drip line/branch tips. Build a retaining wall to protect the rootball and prevent

29

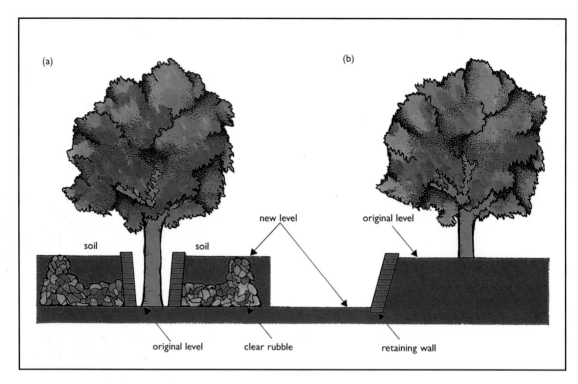

*Fig 23 Changing ground level around trees: (a) Raising ground level;
(b) Lowering ground level.*

soil being washed away. Carry out this work when the tree is dormant or growth at a very low ebb.

When intent on raising levels, first remove any planting from beneath the tree. Then spread coarse gravel over the entire root area to marry up with the revised surroundings. Where levels are to be raised no more than 3–4in (8–10cm) then soil can be used. Depths of soil greater than this can, and will, suffocate the roots.

Container trees ** Extra care is needed between autumn and spring unless trees are to suffer from wind and cold. They need winter shelter and root protection. See page 50.

Where much of the old potting compost has disappeared, leaving half-empty containers, top-dress with fresh before the onset of winter. Where trees are unthrifty or pot bound – are thick roots coming out of the base? Repotting

into a similar-sized container after limited root pruning, is advisable. Where practical, trees can, of course, be potted on into larger-sized containers at this juncture.

Care of New Trees – Extra Work

Push on with all preparatory work in readiness for autumn, early winter or spring planting. Follow up the work of the summer scene.

Drainage ** On heavy soils and in low-lying gardens, the ground can all too easily become waterlogged in wet weather, unless preventive steps are taken. Deal with drainage before rather than after planting.

In small gardens, the construction of one or more rubble-filled sumps will usually be sufficient to prevent future problems. The possible exception is where the garden collects water from

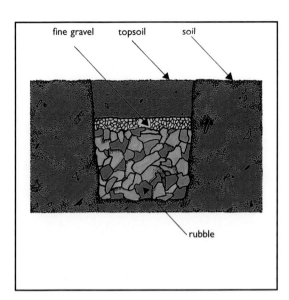

Fig 24   Sump drain.

Fig 25   The stag's horn sumach, Rhus typhina, is easily recognized by its striking large pinnate leaves which colour up well in autumn.

adjoining ground. Here, raised beds are a better proposition.

Position a sump drain in a low spot, near where a tree is to be planted.

Construction of a sump drain. During dry weather, dig out a hole about 3ft (90cm) square and to a similar depth, stacking the topsoil to one side and disposing of the subsoil. Fill the hole to within about 12in (30cm) of the top with clean, broken rubble, consolidating by tamping as filling proceeds. Top over the rubble with a 1½in (4cm) layer of fine gravel to prevent the soil washing down. Finish off with good topsoil to just above the surrounding surface; this is to allow for settlement.

Soil improvements ** As with drainage and levelling, make improvements to soil before rather than after planting. In beds and borders where the soil texture is deemed to be un-satisfactory – no matter whether too heavy or too light – work in plenty of organic matter. Think in terms of applying peat, well-rotted manure or garden compost at the rate of two bucketfuls per sq yd (m).

On heavy soils work in an equivalent amount of coarse sand in addition. Combined with the organic matter this will open up the soil to im-prove both texture and drainage.

When it comes to light sandy soils, organic matter helps to retain moisture and nutrients, so conferring increased drought resistance on trees during long spells of dry weather.

Liming acid clay soils will improve the texture as well as the nutrient status. But be cautious where lime haters like parrotia and liquidambar are to be grown.

Raised beds and tree boxes ** There is still time to construct raised beds – but don't delay. As already mentioned, raised beds are one answer to wet or otherwise unsuitable soil. Consider them, too, as a not unattractive garden feature in their own right.

Also, push ahead with the completion of any tree boxes. These are designed to restrict the root run of trees in confined spaces near drains and building foundations.

Shed storage ** If trees are delivered when the soil is frozen or waterlogged, stand them in a cool, airy but frost-free shed. Loosen any wrap-

31

pings around the stems; this enables air to circulate and so reduces the risk of fungal diseases taking hold. Don't disturb the roots unless the delay is going to be more than a week. Then check for signs of drying out; water only sparingly. On very frosty nights cover over the roots with layers of newspaper.

Planting ** The period from September to November is an ideal time to plant out container-grown trees.

Mulching ** Apply a surface, protective winter mulch around the roots of frost-tender young trees such as magnolia.

TREEWORK

Routine General Care

Don't take needless risks. Never try pruning or lopping in high winds or in slippery, icy conditions. Also avoid working when the chances of success are far from good. For instance, branches will invariably split if attacked with a pruning saw during hard frosts.

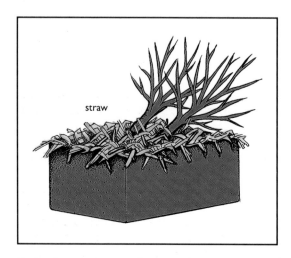

Fig 26   Pre-planting care. Trees delivered during frost are best stored under cover. Untie the tops to allow air circulation. Protect roots with straw or newspaper.

Fig 27   Liquidambar styraciflua with its palmate five-fingered leaves and warm, glowing, autumn tints, bears a strong resemblance to a large Japanese maple (Acer).

Tree supports ** Examine tree ties and supports. Slacken off those which are too tight and liable to cut into the bark. Slipping ties cause chafing, and any play increases the risk of snapping of slender young trunks. So take up any slack.

Check stakes for movement. Also look for signs of rot at soil level. When standard trees are well established and rootfirm, remove stakes complete with ties; they are no longer needed.

Look to wall ties, wires and trellis.

Removal of suckers ** As for summer.

Removal of seedheads ** Pick off poisonous laburnum seed pods if young children are to play in the garden.

Pruning and training ** Cut out dead, damaged or badly diseased wood. Shorten back crossing and inward growing branches.

32

Fig 28 *Crown raising. Remove the lower tree branches. This lets in more light and air near ground level – a good idea for small gardens.*

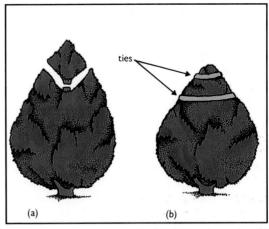

Fig 29 *Heading back: (a) Reduce height by not more than one-third, leaving the cut concealed; (b) Tie in the upper branches to hide the wound and to keep the tree in shape.*

Remedial work: Lop large limbs where necessary.
Crown thinning: Cut out weak, overcrowded and badly placed branches to let in more light and air to the crown of deciduous trees which have obviously been neglected and where the flowering is suffering.
Crown raising: Remove the bottom branches of both deciduous and evergreen trees to leave more headroom for underplanting and to improve air circulation.
Heading back: Shorten back the tips of main leaders and branches to reduce tree size or height of deciduous varieties.
Tying in: At first signs of spread, encircle and tie in multi-stemmed trees to prevent snow and rain forcing branches apart. Conifers are most at risk. Make the ties as inconspicuous as possible using green plastic-coated wire.
Propping and bracing: Trees with large, heavy limbs, that are healthy but liable to break, can often be helped by propping and bracing. See page 48.
Container trees: With all container trees, and bonsai in particular, light pruning at this time is beneficial. Nip back to shorten new growths.

The purpose is not only to tidy up and shape, but also to reduce the area exposed to wind, so cutting down water loss and wind rocking during winter. This is particularly important with evergreens.
Wall-trained trees: Tie in and train ornamentals.

NOTE: Prune trees like birch, poplar and walnut at leaf fall. They bleed badly if left until later winter.

Bark tracing * As for summer.

Propagation ** Many trees are propagated during autumn, and a variety of methods are used.

Take hardwood cuttings of such as mulberry, tamarisk and willow. Root in sheltered positions either outdoors or under a cold frame.

Semi-ripe cuttings of conifers including cypress, juniper, yew and thuja, if taken during September, will root in a heated propagator.

Collect and sow seeds of trees like maple, dogwood, hazel, cotoneaster, hawthorn and liquidambar, plus some varieties of rowan and whitebeam. Overwinter under a vermin-proof cold frame.

Layering is possible with a few trees. Dogwood, hazel, liquidambar and magnolia are worth a try, provided there are branches within easy reach of soil level to peg down.

Rooted suckers of trees like sumach and false acacia can be carefully dug up and replanted or potted up. If potted, give winter protection – all young stock are more at risk in containers than when planted direct into the ground.

Pest and disease control ** Ornamental peach and almond are vulnerable to attacks of peach leaf curl, and should be sprayed with a suitable fungicide at leaf fall.

Care of New Trees – Extra Work

Initial pruning ** At planting time, many deciduous trees need to have their branches shortened by a half to encourage new growth.

Remove the 'feathers' from the stems of young standard trees.

Fig 30 Initial pruning. Before planting, cut back any damaged roots to sound tissue. Shorten the new wood by ⅓ to ½ where a vigorous framework of branches is the aim.

Supporting trees ** Put up all tree stakes, supports, eyehooks and wires before planting. Tie in trees to their supports as soon as they are planted firmly in position.

Wind shelter ** Protect newly planted trees, especially conifers, from cold, drying winds by putting up fine mesh netting screens.

Frost protection ** Give newly potted young trees extra protection in frosty weather. When frost threatens, close the lights on those under frames. Then shade from morning sun to avoid a rapid thaw.

WHICH TREE?

Nursery-Trained Forms

Free-standing trees

Free-standing trees are ultimately grown without permanent ties and supports. Most are catalogued either as bush, standard or multi-stemmed.

Bush trees When offered for sale, have a bushy crown of branches atop a short main trunk, about 12–24in (30–60cm) in height. They make compact trees for small gardens where underplanting is not required.

Standard trees Have a single clear stem/trunk of anything from 3–7ft (1–2m) in height. All are topped with a framework of branches. They come as: short standards (and the same remarks apply to these as to bush trees); half-standards which make intermediate trees in every respect; and full standards which give height and shade. Weeping trees with their pendulous or downswept branches are most likely to be sold as standards or half-standards.

Multi-stemmed trees Live up to their name, and have more than one main stem/trunk – a

Fig 31 *The bright scarlet berries of the evergreen Cotoneaster x hybridus 'Pendulus' provide valuable colour during autumn and winter.*

characteristic which is found more frequently among conifers than among deciduous trees.

Intensive wall-trained trees

There are a number of distinct and recognizable forms of intensive wall-trained trees.

Fan Typically has branches which radiate from the top of a short trunk. Although more commonly reserved for edible varieties of peach and pear, some ornamentals like the flowering almond grow well as fans.

Espalier A short, vertical main trunk, with pairs of branches arranged herringbone fashion is typical. As with fans, more edible fruits are grown this way than ornamentals. Laburnum, however, looks good as an espalier.

Consider the Roots

Container-grown trees

Most trees sold are now container grown. Look for well-rooted trees which are firmly established and anchored in their containers. Be wary of any which are loose and flop about. Avoid trees which are damaged or pot bound, with thick roots growing out of the bottom of the container. Be on guard against trees which are wilting and steer clear of any where the potting compost has dried out and shrunk away from the container sides.

PLANTING TREES

Planting Dates

Deciduous trees Deciduous trees are traditionally planted when leafless/dormant – during autumn and mild winter spells. This is still the best time for the majority. However, when container grown, deciduous trees can be successfully planted out at most times of year, provided soil and weather conditions are reasonable. But it is best to avoid the height of summer and the depths of winter. Generally speaking, trees planted in spring are going to need more attention when it comes to watering and shelter, to see them through their first season. They have little chance to become established before the onset of drying spring winds. The exception to the rule is on heavy clay soil when spring is the better time for planting – puddling can be devastating to roots not firmly anchored.

Broadleaved evergreens and conifers These are ideally planted in autumn or spring. Out of season planting of container-raised trees during late spring and late summer is possible provided they are nursed along afterwards.

The Siting of Trees

As a general rule of thumb guide, don't plant any tree closer to buildings than a distance equal to

Fig 32   Trained tree forms: (a) Bush; (b) Half standard; (c) Standard;
(d) Weeping standard; (e) Fan; (f) Oblique cordon; (g) Espalier.

Fig 33 Buying trees: (a) Container-grown tree; (b) Balled roots (usually conifers if not in containers); (c) Bare-rooted tree removed from its plastic bag (usually deciduous).

its expected ultimate height. This is considered safe for all but the most vigorous rooted willows and poplars. Give these more space. Or better still, opt for alternatives in small gardens. If you plant any closer you risk expensive root damage to foundations. Similarly, keep trees well away from drains and services. Wall-trained ornamentals are the exceptions, provided they are kept well pruned. But avoid planting any closer than 9–12in (23–30cm), for the mutual benefit of walls, buildings and trees. The soil at the base of walls dries out very rapidly, making trees difficult to establish and they are subsequently likely to suffer in prolonged drought. Plant any closer to a building than 12in (30cm) and the stability of the tree comes into question, too – they are very difficult to support.

Damage to foundations Damage to foundations can be caused directly or indirectly.
Direct damage: Is brought about when small roots work their way into the crevices in founda-

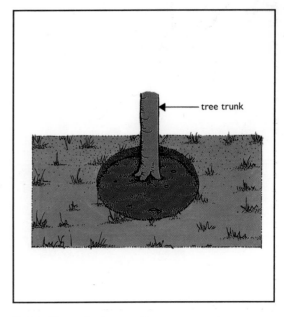

Fig 34 Tree collar in grass. Keep a grass- and weed-free area around the base of newly planted trees.

37

Fig 35 Parrotia persica *produces masses of bright red flowers on bare branches each spring – in addition to attractive autumn leaf tints.*

tions. As they grow they gradually force the cracks to widen. Over the years the foundations disintegrate. The secondary effects of cracked walls letting in damp and frost all too often follow. *Indirect damage:* Can be caused on any soil, but it is most serious on 'heavy' soil and on 'made up' land. Heavy soils expand when wet and contract when drying. Since this movement takes place over the entire length or width of the building, little damage is done. However, immediately tree roots come into the calculations, things can be serious. Tree roots take up a considerable amount of moisture; this brings about uneven drying out and differential settlement of the subsoil – the start of many structural problems.

Tree box In gardens where trees cannot be grown without the risk of damage to drains, underground services and foundations, root restriction provides one answer. The most popular method is to use containers (see page

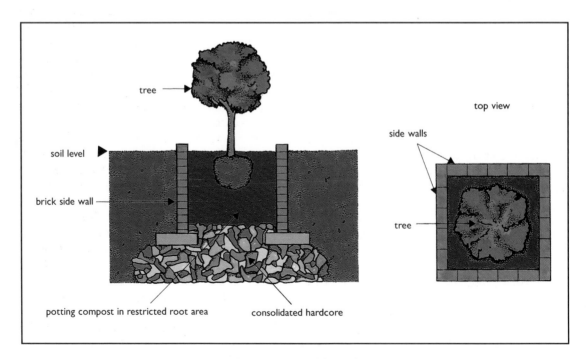

Fig 36 *Tree box.*

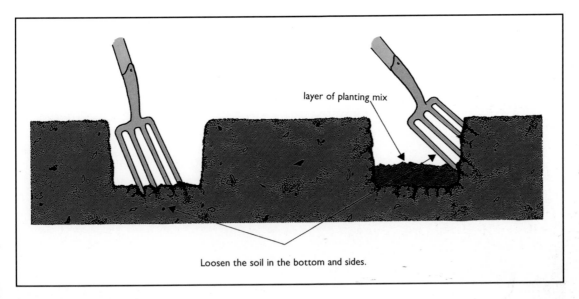

layer of planting mix

Loosen the soil in the bottom and sides.

Fig 37 Preparing the planting pocket.

57). Tree boxes are a useful alternative. Choosing a spot where there is no likelihood of interfering with underground services, dig out a hole about 4ft (1.2m) square and 3ft (90cm) deep. Stack topsoil to one side. Lay and consolidate a 4in (10cm) layer of rubble in the bottom. Then, with the help of wooden shuttering, lay a 3in (7.5cm) thick and 12in (30cm) wide bed of concrete around the outer edge of the rubble raft. Finally build a single course wall – 4½in (11cm) thick – to form a square box some 30in (75cm) deep with outside measurements of 3×3ft (90×90cm). The top of the box should be level with the surrounding soil or paving. Fill the completed box with topsoil and plant in a pocket of planting mixture.

Planting pockets Garden trees are best planted out into pockets, no matter whether planting into raised beds, boxes, borders, lawns or paved areas (where the odd paving slab has been lifted). When planting in grass first strip off the turf.

Dig out planting pockets at least twice as wide as the root spread in the case of lifted trees; or double rootball width with container-grown stock. Make the holes at least half as deep again

as the root run or rootball. Stack the topsoil to one side. Loosen the bottom and sides of the hole with a garden fork to relieve possible soil compaction. This will assist tree roots to grow into the surrounding soil more quickly. Fork plenty of peat, well-rotted garden compost or manure into the bottom of the pocket, working in a handful of bonemeal at the same time. If the soil is very impoverished, mix in a small handful of John Innes base fertilizer or Growmore along with the bonemeal.

Before planting, drench the rootball of container and balled trees, and allow to drain for at least an hour before attempting to remove from their containers/nets. Soak bare-root trees in a bucket/tank of clean water.

Try tree roots for size in the planting pocket, and make any necessary adjustments. Allow for bedding on about 2in (5cm) of topsoil/planting mixture. Bear in mind that the tree should be finally left at the same depth as before the move.

Stakes for free-standing trees are best hammered home before planting, so avoiding possible injury to tree roots afterwards. Supports for wall-trained trees should also be in position before planting. See page 46.

LEAF TINTS, FRUITS AND BERRIES

Broadleaved trees		
Acer palmatum and varieties	Japanese Maple	Lf
Amelanchier lamarckii	Snowy Mespilus	Lf
Arbutus unedo	Strawberry Tree	Fruit
Betula pendula and varieties	Birch	Lf
Cercidiphyllum japonicum	Katsura Tree	Lf
Cercis siliquastrum	Judas Tree	Seed pods
Cornus mas	Cornelian Cherry (Dogwood)	Lf and Berry
Crataegus prunifolia	Plum-leaf Thorn	Lf and Berry
Gleditsia triacanthos 'Sunburst'	Honey Locust	Lf
Koelreuteria paniculata and varieties	Golden Rain Tree	Lf
Liquidambar styraciflua	Liquidambar	Lf
Malus and varieties	Apple	Fruit
Malus and varieties	Flowering Crab	Fruit
Rhus typhina	Stag's Horn Sumach	Lf
Sorbus aria and varieties	Whitebeam	Lf and Berry
Sorbus aucuparia	Mountain Ash	Lf and Berry
Conifers		
Cryptomeria japonica 'Elegans'	Japanese Cedar	Lf
Ginkgo bilaba	Maidenhair Tree	Lf

Setting the Trees

Container-grown trees in rigid containers
Remove containers before lowering tree into hole. Where roots are matted, gently tease some out. Trim back any which are damaged.

Container-grown trees in floppy containers
Cut away the container after the tree is positioned in the hole.

After trees are positioned, gradually fill up the planting holes, firming soil or planting mix between roots and sides of the pocket as work proceeds. A good planting mixture can be prepared by mixing one part each of sand and peat with 3 parts good topsoil – all parts by bulk. Mix in a handful each of bonemeal and Growmore per bucketful of mix. Check the tree is at the same depth as before, or only a shade deeper – no more than about ¾in (2cm). Tie trees to their supports. Water generously to settle the soil. Complete any top pruning. See page 66.

NOTE: Where trees are planted against a wall or in very sandy soil, deep watering can save the day. Insert one or two drain-pipes vertically, near the trunk, before infilling the planting pocket. Small stones are fed into the drain-pipe, and planting mix packed around pipe and roots. Subsequently, water is poured down the pipe until it overflows. Repeat at regular intervals, up to two or three times a day during dry weather when trying to get trees established.

When planting trees for screening and shelter it is a good idea to set them close and remove alternate plants later. Or, interplant chosen varieties with quick growing inexpensive varieties like cherry, plum, maple, cypress or tamarisk with the idea of removing later, having had the advantage of a quick shelter/screen.

CHAPTER 4

Winter – December to February

Outdoor work on garden trees is still possible in winter, although frequently hampered by unfavourable soil and weather conditions. High winds, frosts and snow, combined with short, gloomy days and lack of warm sun are no encouragement to gardeners – work becomes uncomfortable and difficult.

December is generally cold. Even if the weather is fine and bright, the soil is likely to be too wet, frozen or snow covered either to walk over or work. January is usually the coldest month

Fig 38 A well grown Cornus mas when leafless and in full flower becomes a misty golden haze in winter sun.

of the year. Gales, storms, rain and frost make work outdoors impractical and unsafe. Snowfalls are often heavy and persist for long periods. It is a time to give outdoor trees at risk all the protection possible. February is often a varied month – with the differences between areas becoming more pronounced. In mild districts, as the days start to lengthen, it is not uncommon for buds on trees such as cherry and plum to swell visibly and bring a hint of spring. Meanwhile, cold areas – on high ground and in northern districts – are usually still in the grips of winter. The weather may be just as severe as January, with lingering keen frosts and heavy snowfalls. Elsewhere, expect something of a mixed bag, ranging from harsh midwinter conditions to those of a more moderate late winter/early spring clime.

GROUNDWORK

Routine General Care

End of season clean up **

Push ahead as for autumn whenever conditions allow. Aim to complete all the work by January.

Disposal of leaves and garden waste **

In small gardens, getting rid of any quantity of leaves, prunings, weeds and the like, frequently presents something of a problem.

41

Healthy fallen leaves Those from deciduous trees are best composted. It is wasteful to burn them or to cart them to the local tip, unless pest or disease ridden. Make them into garden compost and so enable valuable organic matter to be returned to the soil. When well rotted, leaf compost is applied mainly as a topdressing in spring. It is also useful at planting time and for digging into borders. The ideal is to keep leaves separate from other waste garden vegetation, and to compost them into leaf mould. However, in practice, more often than not, they are composted in the main bin along with grass clippings, vegetable waste, less noxious weeds and the like. The main objection to including leaves in the general compost bin is that they tend to slow down the rotting of the bulk of the compost.

Making leaf compost/mould Although leaves can be stacked in open heaps, it is much better to contain them, if for no other reason than for the sake of neatness. Make a wire mesh holder of convenient size – say, 4ft (1.2m) square and 3ft (90cm) high. The size will obviously need to be geared to the quantity of leaves involved. Galvanized or plastic-coated wire mesh netting, fixed on to a light frame of some sort will suffice. Into the bottom, spread a 2in (5cm) layer of coarse bark chippings, shredded wood, gravel or small stones for drainage. This is advisable in all gardens, but vital if the underlying soil is inclined to be heavy and slow draining. Pile in a 6in (15cm) layer of moist leaves. Lightly firm, then sprinkle on a small handful of Growmore fertilizer per sq yd (m), or use proprietary activator as the makers recommend. Follow with a scattering of topsoil, then more leaves, followed by more fertilizer/activator and soil. And so on, building up the heap as the leaves are swept up.

Protect the heaps from rain, to prevent loss of nutrients and to hasten rotting. Heavy duty plastic sheet, well anchored, is ideal for the purpose. In anything from twelve to twenty-four months the leaves will have rotted down into a fibrous brown, flaky, sweet-smelling mass ready for use. Fork the well-rotted leaf compost out at the bottom, while continuing to layer up leaves at the top.

Rotting can be speeded up – but only slightly – by forking or turning the heap two or three times at monthly intervals. However, turning a heap is hard work, not essential and rarely attempted. It has the added disadvantage of having to complete each heap in one go. When the bulk of leaves is substantial, have two heaps – build up one as the other rots down. When composting leaves in the main bin, omit the soil.

Prunings Take up a lot of space, are bulky to carry to the tip, and can be a source of infection if left lying around. Prunings are not always easy to burn, and not all local byelaws permit the lighting of bonfires. One way to minimize the problem of light prunings, up to ¾in (2cm) in diameter, is to hire, borrow or buy a compost shredder. Powered versions are the better bet, being quick and efficient, though expensive. Manual shredders can be very strenuous to work and are time consuming. Prunings, fed into a hopper at the top, are chopped and the shredded material comes out at the bottom. Some of these shredders are fitted with collecting bags.

Shredding greatly reduces the bulk and, once shredded, healthy prunings can then be composted in much the same way as leaves. The limiting factor is the proportion of evergreen prunings from trees such as conifers. No more than about 10 per cent is recommended, otherwise the compost will be slow to rot. Where it is estimated that between 10 per cent and 20 per cent evergreens make up the bulk of the shredded prunings, the shreddings can be applied direct as a mulch. The point to watch here is that undecomposed mulches are going to rot down, and in so doing will rob the soil of nitrogen. The most successful way to remedy this is by giving the soil an extra spring dressing such as Growmore to compensate. Prunings with over 20 per cent of evergreens are best carted to the tip, along with prickly kinds like holly and any suspected of harbouring disease.

Tree stumps and heavy branches   It may well be possible to dry off, saw up and burn any timber, along with diseased material. Where burning is practical, and permitted, an incinerator of the lidded bin type is preferable to the wire mesh box type. They produce less smoke and have a greater life expectancy. However, where there is a lot of heavy, bulky, or wet material – as when initially clearing out a neglected garden – it is often easier and cheaper in the long run, to hire a skip.

Root pruning **

Complete the root pruning of over-vigorous and unproductive flowering ornamental trees by the end of December in the south, and early December in cold districts. See page 27.

Undercutting **

By mid-December finish the preparation of established trees which are to be lifted and transplanted in twelve to twenty-four months' time. See page 27.

Lifting and transplanting **

Established trees which have been prepared previously for the move should be established in their new positions by mid-December in more southerly areas and by early December in northern areas.

Feeding **

Finish off any boring and topdressing of old trees by the end of December.

Care of New Trees – Extra Work

Preplanting preparations **

If and when conditions allow, continue to carry out preparations for planting and soil improvements.

Planting **

During mild spells, continue to set out new deciduous trees.

Root protection **

Apply mulch, or renew the autumn surface mulch, around newly planted trees known to have frost-tender roots. Or peg down a generous layer of straw. Pay particular attention to young potted trees.

Young stock **

Protect seeds/seedlings in frames. Pick over cuttings and dust with fungicide at the first signs of trouble.

Refirm **

As soon as the thaws come, refirm the roots of any trees lifted by frost or wind. Cover over any exposed roots with fine topsoil.

TREEWORK

Routine General Care

Tree supports and ties **

Carry out a routine inspection as for autumn.

Removal of suckers **

Continue the ongoing task of pulling/cutting away suckers.

Pruning, training and lopping **

Push ahead with any unfinished work left over from autumn. Aim to complete any hard cutting back – including crown raising, thinning and heading back and lopping – by late December in mild areas and by mid-January in cold districts.

43

Trees suffer less setbacks if this is done before the sap starts to rise.

Propagation **

Sow seeds of broadleaved deciduous trees like apple and pear, and of conifers including cedar, fir and thuja. Chill the sown pots of seed in the fridge, or in a vermin-proof cold frame, for six to eight weeks. Only then move into the warmth to germinate.

Detach, lift and plant out suckers of false acacia, choosing a sheltered spot outdoors. Alternatively, pot them up and overwinter under a cold frame.

Take hardwood cuttings of mulberry and willow. Root in a sheltered garden border – or, preferably, under the protection of a cold frame.

Semi-ripe cuttings of cypress will root in warmth, if taken in January.

Pest and disease control **

There is still time to spray almond and peach against peach leaf curl disease, using a copper or other suitable fungicide – but don't delay beyond late December.

Care of New Trees – Extra Work

Support, stake, tie and prune **

Support, stake, tie and prune trees as they are planted. See page 34.

Tree guards **

Tree guards are invaluable to protect small young trees – most especially in the 'hungry' months against rabbits in rural areas.

Winter protection **

Replace or readjust as necessary any netting or screening erected around newly planted trees in autumn to shelter against wind. Many trees are at risk from keen frosts, so increase protection before the onset of the most severe weather. Pay particular attention to trees growing in containers. Knock heavy snowfalls off evergreens.

SUPPORTING TREES

Trees vary in their need for support. This need is largely determined by age, variety, form, situation and use.

Nursery Trees

Very young trees which are in the process of developing a basic trunk and branch framework, prior to final planting out, must have firm support. Although normally in the province of the commercial grower raising plants for sale, this point is mentioned here for the benefit of the enthusiast set on propagating trees.

Young deciduous trees with a single, supple main stem, should be given support early in life – to ensure a straight trunk later. In the case of trees up to about 18in (45cm) in height a split cane and ties will suffice. Taller trees up to about 4ft (1.2m) in height need more substantial support. For supports, use heavy-grade bamboo canes, tubular metal 'grow-sticks' or short bean poles, making sure they are not too heavy and clumsy. When buying any support, remember to allow adequate extra length for the part buried below ground. Think in terms of at least a quarter of the total being buried.

Use soft twine to tie a young tree as inconspicuously as possible to its support. Leave a small amount of slack to allow for some growth without strangling the stem.

Where several young trees are being grown, seriously consider providing extra post and wire support. This applies especially to trees growing in pots – they are liable to blow over. Insert timber or metal stakes, no more than 7–10ft (2–3m) apart. Secure a single strand of 12 or 14 gauge wire between the stakes, stretched horizontally about 4ft (1.2m) above ground. Line out the pots and tie the individual canes to the wire.

Stakes and Ties

Stakes Bush and standard trees are normally supported with pointed timber stakes. The preferred timbers are chestnut, oak and ash. These are more durable than the widely available softwoods like larch. All timber stakes will last longer if treated with a safe horticultural preservative like 'Cuprinol' before use.

Timber stakes come in various shapes and sizes. Some are sawn and squared of regular thickness; others are peeled, rounded and slightly tapered. Sawn timber is generally easier to handle, but peeled timber is perhaps more natural and pleasing to look at. Avoid badly knotted timbers which are more vulnerable to snapping than sound wood. When buying timber stakes, always relate thickness to length. If too thin they are likely to snap off during a heavy storm.

Metal tree stakes are more durable, but less attractive than timber. There is also a real risk of chafing of the bark, creating easy entry areas for pests and diseases.

Ties Although there are numerous makes of proprietary tree ties on the market, most are variations of two main types.

The first is the 'nail on' type, consisting of a broad, flat plastic or canvas strip, together with a spacer to keep the trunk from rubbing against the stake. See illustration. The method of fixing is to nail one end of the tie to the stake at the required height. Then thread the other end through the spacer, around the back of the tree

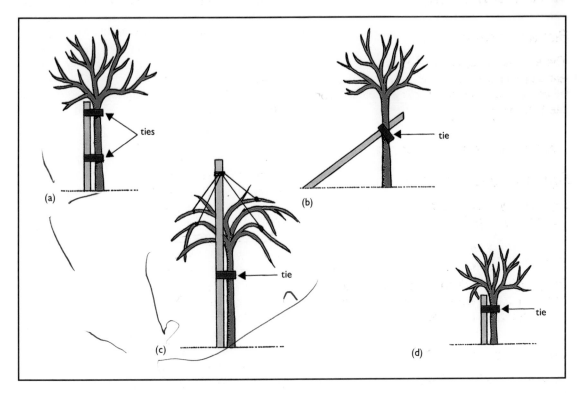

Fig 39   Methods of tree support: (a) Ordinary vertical stake; (b) Oblique stake; (c) Tall vertical maypole stake; (d) Short stake.

trunk, returning it through the spacer again. The tie is pulled tight with the free end, and finally nailed to the stake, making sure the spacer is firmly in place between the trunk and stake. Being nailed to the stake there is no problem of the tie slipping down. However, further adjustments are slow, necessitating the removal of the nail. The danger of splitting the stake is increased with each adjustment.

The second version of the tie is the 'adjustable buckle', the essential difference being in the final fixing. The loose end of the tie band is finally threaded through a buckle instead of being nailed. This allows the tie to be quickly and easily adjusted.

Staking and Tying

Wherever possible, aim to fix stakes into place after the planting hole has been dug out, but

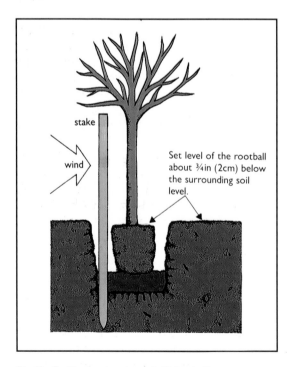

Fig 40 Positioning tree in a pit. Drive in the stake slightly off-centre facing into the direction of the prevailing wind.

stake

wind

Set level of the rootball about ¾in (2cm) below the surrounding soil level.

before the tree is lowered into position. Otherwise, there is a risk of damage to delicate roots if stakes are hammered home after planting.

Fix trees ties after covering over the roots and the final firming in – to allow for any settlement during planting.

Standard trees – vertical stake A single vertical stake is the most popular and widely used way to support ornamental standard trees. A good general rule when using single vertical stakes is to set them into the planting holes slightly off centre, ideally into the direction of the prevailing wind. The purpose of this is so that the tree is blown away from the stake rather than towards it. This minimizes the risk of rubbing and chafing of the bark. Select a stake to match the tree – the top of the stake needs to be about 2in (5cm) below the point where the lowest branch joins the trunk. Be sure to saw off the top if the stake is too long. Otherwise, there is a risk of chafing of the lower branches. Secure the trunk to the stake with one tree tie near the top of the support and with a second about half-way down.

Standard trees – oblique stake This method of staking scores in exposed gardens with an above average expectation of strong winds. It will enable a tree to withstand the buffeting from gales much more effectively than a single vertical stake.

Hammer the stake into the ground at an oblique angle of about 45 degrees, driving in the point some distance from the planting hole. The top of the stake should face into the direction of the prevailing wind, and come at least three-quarters of the way up the trunk. After planting, fasten the trunk to the stake, where the two meet, using a single tie. See illustration.

Standard trees – twin stakes When planting larger than average, extra heavy trees, with a well-developed crown and big rootball, twin stakes come into their own. In practice it can be difficult getting a single stake close enough in to the trunk. This is also an excellent method to use after lifting and transplanting established trees into new positions.

Drive in the twin stakes, one at each side of the planting hole, so that the rootball will comfortably fit between them. Bolt on a horizontal cross rail. Fix one end to each stake, at a height just sufficient to leave a 3in (8cm) clearance under the lowest branches.

Attach the trunk securely to the cross rail with a single tie, after first wrapping the trunk with protective bands of sacking to prevent the cross timber rail rubbing the trunk.

Bush trees – vertical stake A short vertical stake is the usual method of support for bush forms of ornamental trees. The stake should be of sufficient length to take it up to just above the bottom two or three branches. Fix the tree to its support by means of a single tie fairly near the top.

Wall-trained Trees

Wires and wall fixings rank with the most popular and effective means of support for ornamentals trained on walls.

The aim is to arrange strands of 10 gauge galvanized wire horizontally, about 16in (40cm) apart up to a height of 10ft (3m) – or less, depending on wall height. Drill and plug the wall, then screw in vine eyes – one to hold each end of individual strands, plus additional eyes at 7ft (2m) intervals on long runs. Galvanized screw-type vine eyes make a highly serviceable and economic wall fixing. Straining bolts fixed at one end of each wire will make a neat job of tightening up while preventing any subsequent sagging.

Guying

When carefully carried out, guying gives good all-round resistance to wind, from any point of the compass. It provides a most effective means of support for a tall tree, with a strong central trunk, reaching over 10ft (3m) at the time of planting.

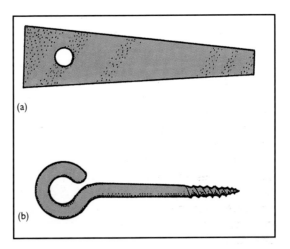

Fig 41 Methods of tree support – wall fixings:
(a) Flat vine eye; (b) Eyelet vine eye.

Only professional gardeners would be attempting to plant out trees of this size, but guying is mentioned here since it is also a practical way to stabilize an old tree.

Basically three, or more, guy wires/cords are fixed to the main trunk – high up in the tree just above a branch. The free ends are pulled taut and attached to pegs hammered into the ground, spaced around the tree equidistant from each other. To prevent debarking, the wires are threaded through the likes of short lengths of hose pipe.

Either buy a complete guying kit which comes complete with instructions, or improvise. In the latter case, three 6in (15cm) lengths of durable ½in (1cm) hose, three lengths of No 14 gauge wire or nylon cord and three hardwood or metal guying pegs up to 2ft (60cm) or more in length will be needed.

Thread one end of each wire through a length of hose, until at least 6in (15cm) shows. Bend them round into 'U' shapes. Loop each over a branch and around the main trunk, twisting to secure. Pull each wire taut and attach it to its appropriate peg. Try to ensure there is an even tension on each wire and that the wires are pulled out at an angle of 45 degrees. Position the pegs where they are least likely to get in the way.

47

Check wires and ties regularly, keeping a special watch on nylon cords which can slacken off.

Supporting Old Trees

For those who are faced with the problem of retaining an old tree under a statutory tree preservation order – or who want to save a tree of outstanding beauty and character – 'bracing' can provide one solution. This is a job normally best left to qualified tree surgeons. It should not be attempted by the inexperienced because of the possible safety hazards involved, and because it is a job which calls for considerable 'know-how' and experience. In essence, bracing involves letting eyelets into large branches which are then braced together – or to the main trunk – by means of a strong cable to prevent them falling outwards in high winds or during heavy snowfalls. All suspect limbs must be adequately secured.

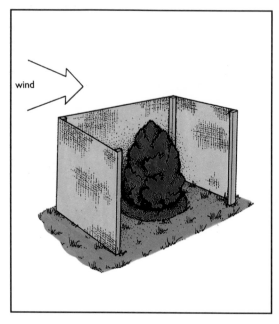

Fig 42 · Tree protection – temporary windbreak. Fine mesh netting screen on a light frame gives protection against the prevailing wind on the exposed side.

THE YEAR-ROUND PROTECTION OF TREES

Young nursery stock, new transplants and container trees are often inadvertently put at risk by unfavourable growing conditions. The main factors most likely to cause harm are environmental – leaving leeway for improvements. Extremes of wind, sun, shade, frost, rain and drought are all to be avoided.

Wind

The main danger period for young trees is from late autumn through to late spring, when cold drying winds cause leaf scorch and drying out. Newly planted trees – evergreens are particularly at risk – need immediate shelter. This is vital in exposed gardens. Screens with about 50 per cent permeability – such as hedging and fine mesh netting – allow some air to filter through and are preferable to impermeable barriers like solid walling. At times, solid walls will create severe and harmful turbulence.

Single trees: Are fairly easily protected from the full force of wind by encircling with fine mesh netting, or hessian, supported on canes or a light temporary frame. Netting is the better bet. It allows more light to reach the foliage than hessian, is longer lasting and more pleasing to the eye. Such screens need to be at least as tall as the tree. When providing protection for evergreens it is important not to smother the tree, or to prevent light from reaching its lower leaves in particular, if bareness is to be avoided.

Groups or rows: Where trees have been planted in groups or rows, it is a good idea to provide shelter on the windward side. In such a situation, fine mesh netting, hessian or wattle screens, attached to stout posts, will serve the purpose well. When protecting a wide bed of, say, dwarf conifers, bear in mind that a long screen across the direction of the wind will protect a level area four to six times its height. Reckon on a 5ft (1.5m) high screen protecting a newly planted 20ft (6m) wide border. The best long-term answer to protecting dwarf and slow-growing trees in windswept gardens is to grow a permanent hedge or screen, provided space will allow. Larch, birch and flowering plum are hard to beat for a quick shelter, becoming effective within two to three years. Beech, hornbeam, field maple, cypress and flowering cherry are other good shelter-belt trees. Allow them about five years to become fully effective.

Container trees: Tress growing in immovable containers are treated in a similar manner to the single trees. Move those in smaller containers close up to a sheltered house wall.

Frost and Snow

Frost-sensitive roots   One way to protect trees like magnolias in their first year, is to cover their frost-tender roots with a generous 4–6in (10–15cm) layer of straw or leaves, held firmly in place with pegged-down netting.

Frozen trees   Never allow frozen trees to thaw out quickly. Shade them until they have thawed. Those in east-facing borders are most at risk. Evergreens, in particular, can suffer irreparable damage by a too rapid thaw in the early morning sun.

Container trees

Small container trees: Move small container trees to sheltered positions, or under cover. Any tree overwintering under cover should be given plenty of ventilation, except during prolonged hard, frosty weather. Trees will benefit from the extra warmth from the house wall which acts very much like a storage heater. Daytime warmth is released, slowly during the night hours. Where a number of containers need to be protected, often the easiest way is to plunge them into a bed of straw or leaves.

Large container trees: If overwintering out-

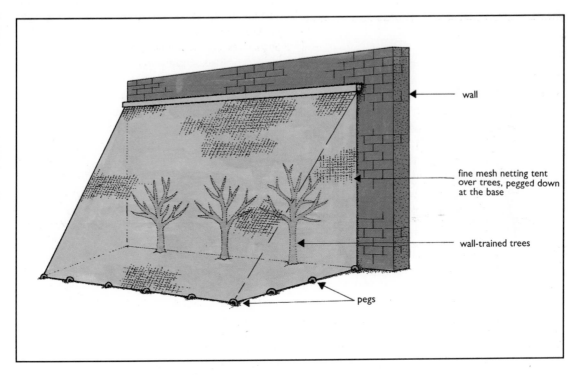

Fig 43   Tree protection – frost protection of wall trees.

wall

fine mesh netting tent over trees, pegged down at the base

wall-trained trees

pegs

Fig 44 The beauty of bark needs to be seen to be appreciated – like the trunk of this old Birch (Betula).

doors, large container trees must have their roots protected from hard frost. Insulate each container with a 6in (15cm) layer of straw or leaves held in place with pinned-down netting or plastic sheet. Cover the sides as well as the top of the rootball.

Snow Knock snow off evergreens after heavy falls.

Sun and Shade

Sun Protect newly planted trees from fierce overhead sun. Evergreens are most at risk. A canopy of fine mesh netting supported on a light frame will provide useful midday shade.

In the south, thin-barked trees like young birch, will benefit from having their trunks wrapped in hessian to give protection from hot, strong sun. This is worthwhile for the first couple of years or so.

Shade Wherever practical, in shaded gardens, paint dark background surfaces white to reflect – rather than absorb – light. Also it helps to give trees a more generous spacing when grown in shade. Don't subject fruiting trees to excessive shade. They need sun during summer and autumn to help ripen young wood, so promoting increased flowers and fruit. The warmth and shelter of a south or west-facing wall is of enormous benefit. Selectively thin out the branches on large trees where they overshadow smaller specimens.

Rain and Drought

Wet and containers Persistent heavy winter rain, without drying sun can leave containers waterlogged for long periods, unless some counter measures are taken. To leave containers outdoors without any overhead protection is asking for trouble. Where there is a roof overhang to intercept some of the rain, moving containers close into a house wall can help considerably, but ensure that none of the trees is going to be splashed by drips from gutters and downspouts. Another alternative is to make

Fig 45 Tree protection. Tie in multi-stemmed conifers to stop them spreading under the weight of the snow.

individual plastic collars for each container to keep the rain of the potting compost, but be vigilant – the containers must not dry out. Make sure also that containers do not stand in water, collecting in such as drip trays. During winter it is especially important to stand containers on a free-draining base..

Dryness Wall-trained and dwarf trees, planted at or near the foot of a wall, are particularly liable to root dryness. This can be a most serious problem for newly planted trees in their first year or two until well established. Drain-pipes, set into the soil, and angled in towards the roots of wall trees – as described on page 40 – is one answer to making watering easier and more effective. Of

course, mulching in summer should be standard practice.

The sinking of one or two large plantpots, up to their rims, near any vulnerable tree, makes deep water penetration more effective, quicker and easier. Simply keep the pots topped up with water in dry weather and the water will seep out naturally. Another trick of the trade is to make a saucer-like depression round the tree trunk. Ridge up the soil in a circle 2ft (60cm) or more out from the trunk. The ridge needs to be at least on line with the branch tips. Water then applied to the tree is trapped by the ridge, and is able to percolate down to do some good. Level off the ridge in autumn, before prolonged wet weather returns, otherwise risk waterlogging.

BARK AND EVERGREEN FOLIAGE

Broadleaved trees		
Arbutus unedo	Strawberry Tree	E
Betula pendula and varieties	Birch	Bk
Cotoneaster × 'Hybridus Pendulus'	Weeping Cotoneaster	E
Eucalyptus niphophila	Snow Gum	Bk and E
Ilex × altaclarensis and varieties	Holly	E
Salix caprea 'Kilmarnock'	Kilmarnock Willow	Bk
Trachycarpus fortunei	Chusan Palm	Bk and E
Conifers		
Abies koreana	Korean Fir	E
Araucaria araucana	Monkey Puzzle	E
Calocedrus decurrens	Incense Cedar	E
Chamaecyparis lawsoniana and varieties	Lawson Cypress	E
Cryptomeria japonica 'Elegans'	Japanese Cedar	E
Cupressocyparis leylandii and varieties	Leyland Cypress	E
Juniperus communis and varieties	Juniper	E
Picea glauca 'Albertiana Conica'	Spruce	E
Pinus mugo	Mountain Pine	E
Taxus baccata 'Standishii'	Golden Yew	E
Thuja occidentalis 'Rheingold'	Arborvitae	E

Bk=Bark interest
E=Evergreen foliage and form interest

CHAPTER 5

Spring – March to May

The weather is likely to be more changeable during the period late winter through to mid-spring than at any other time of the year, and it is difficult to generalize on what to expect. The mix of wind, sun, rain, frost and snow is never the same two years running, or from one part of the country to another, or from one week to the next.

In March, weather can remain cold and wintry,

Fig 46 What Syringa vulgaris (lilac) lacks in fruit or foliage interest is more than made up for with its masses of sweetly-scented spring flowers.

with work and growth virtually at a standstill. On the other hand, it can become sunny and mild, with soil drying out sufficiently to enable work to proceed apace. In warmer areas, expect significant signs of movement and bud burst.

April can be dull, mild and showery, ideal weather to push ahead with the planting out of container-grown trees. But, conversely, it can be dry and sunny by day and frosty by night; at these times newly planted trees are going to need nursing along and protecting.

May is often hot and dry with long periods of sun and high drying winds. On calm, clear nights, radiation frosts can be treacherous, killing off blossoms and wiping out an entire season's fruit crop. The message is straightforward. Be on guard and give protection wherever possible, whenever frost threatens. Drought, too, can become a serious problem with newly planted trees of all kinds. As well as extreme dryness at the roots and drying wind on the foliage, comes the added strain of blazing sun. In some years this can be hotter even than in summer. Again, protection is called for, this time in the form of shading.

GROUNDWORK

Routine General Care

Cultivations *

Take advantage of improved weather. Whenever soil conditions allow, push ahead with all cultivations, lightly working bare soil in the vicinity of trees.

Feeding **

As a general rule, don't feed newly planted ornamental or edible fruit trees for the first two years – apart from those on impoverished ground and sandy soils. Make the roots work. Thereafter, give a light, early spring dressing of general fertilizer like Growmore, spread over the root run prior to mulching. Always make sure the soil is moist before feeding. For acid lovers like firs, magnolia, katsura and parrotia, John Innes base fertilizer is hard to beat. Feeding is particularly important when mature trees, in full bearing, are struggling on light, sandy, hungry soils. For all except surface rooting trees, hoe the dry feed into the top 1in (3cm) or so of soil. To avoid damage to surface rooting magnolias, strawberry trees and conifers, sprinkle the feed over the soil and water in.

Keep a close watch on magnolias and parrotia, especially if the garden overlies chalk or limestone. If they become unthrifty and show characteristic signs of yellowing, suspect chlorosis and give a soil drench of iron 'Sequestrene'.

Consider liquid feeding on light soil as a boost, mainly to young trees. Foliar feeding – where extremely dilute quick-acting feeds are sprayed directly onto leaves – can be useful too, particularly for reviving trees under stress. Use only proprietary feeds specially prepared for the purpose and read instructions carefully. Application rates vary from one make to another. Apply evenly, on a dull day, otherwise you risk leaf scorch.

Application rates of spring topdressings Relate the amount of fertilizer to the type of tree, to its condition, and to the soil. With *ornamental trees* apply a small handful of Growmore or similar per sq yd (m). Where the soil is poor and sandy, increase the dressing by about a quarter. But with heavy applications it is advisable to split the application into two halves, leaving fourteen days between. Alternatively, you can boost the dry feed with several liquid feeds during the summer months.

Container trees Beginning about three weeks after potting or topdressing, give all freely growing container trees a balanced high potash liquid feed, and repeat at three-weekly or monthly intervals.

Mulching **

Once things have warmed up a bit, apply a generous surface mulch to trees, as far as supplies of peat, shredded bark, well-rotted garden compost and manure will permit. In cases of shortages always give priority to newly planted trees. The mulch goes on after the fertilizer topdressing. Hoe off the weeds before mulching. And if the ground is dry – water. The mulch will then help to conserve moisture during the weeks ahead and suppress further weed growth.

Composting *

Continue to build up the compost heap.

Preparation and undercutting *

Complete any unfinished undercutting of established trees which are to be moved in eighteen months time. This is a job best done in autumn.

Lift and transplant *

Lift and transplant established trees undercut some eighteen months ago. Deciduous trees are best moved in autumn.

Topdressing *

Where old trees were fed earlier by boring and topdressing, top up the holes wih potting compost as necessary.

Container trees **

See to potting and topdressing. See page 62. Container trees should never be allowed to dry out completely at any time. Evergreens are particularly at risk, since severe drying invariably results in scorching and loss of foliage. This can be very disfiguring and the damage is usually irreparable. Examine containers daily and water whenever the compost feels dry. If in doubt, newcomers should not hesitate to use a water meter until experience is gained.

Care of New Trees – Extra Work

Soil improvements *

Aim to finish off any soil improvements in preparation for planting. Ideally, work in copious amounts of manure or compost on all soils plus coarse sand to improve the texture of heavy clay soils.

Planting preparations *

Clean up the land, forking out weeds. Apply weedkiller if difficult and persistent weeds like dandelion, dock, nettle, and ground elder are in evidence. It is better to delay planting until autumn than plant on dirty land and to continue working the ground and worrying the weeds throughout summer. Get all drainage work done in good time so as to allow the soil to settle before planting.

Refirming **

Firm in trees lifted by frost or wind and, if necessary, cover over any exposed roots with good topsoil. Keep newly planted trees well watered and weed-free.

Planting **

Prepare planting pockets and set out container-grown trees; this is a good time for conifers and broadleaved evergreens. See page 57. When planting in grass, first cut out and remove a circle of turf. The easiest way to mark out the circle is to hammer in a cane centrally; tie on a length of string half the width of the intended circle; attach a pointed stick; and then pull taut and mark out the circle.

TREEWORK

Routine General Care

Growth can be rapid at this time of year, so don't delay work any longer than absolutely necessary.

Tree stakes and ties *

Continue to keep a close watch and adjust as necessary.

Fig 47 Picea glauca 'Albertiana Conica' is an outstanding choice, slow growing conifer, noted for its vivid green foliage – especially in the spring.

Pruning **

Cut out any dead or diseased wood promptly. Shorten back any frosted tips on deciduous trees, back to sound wood. Cleanly cut off any frozen, blackened buds. Resist the temptation to clip broadleaved evergreens and conifers with scorched or browned foliage – the result of a hard winter. They are best left until summer before neatly removing the worst of the affected foliage.

Give container trees the once-over. Shorten back straggly and untidy shoots along with any which are badly placed.

Trees which are renowned for their bark interest are pruned regularly – mostly in spring, but there are exceptions (see below). The reasons for pruning are two-fold: first, to expose the bark and, second, to stimulate the production of young wood. The young wood is usually the best coloured. Prune in March–April at the latest. Feathers also need to be removed regularly – these are the small shoots which develop mostly towards the top of the trunk, below the main branches.

Alder Winter display of bright orange young wood. Remove lower branches and cut back new growths by three-quarters in spring.

Cedar gum Smooth grey flaking bark. Once trees are two years old, cut back to 6ft (1.8m) above ground each spring.

Chinese red-barked birch Marbled flaking bark in fawn, pink and red. Remove the feathers in autumn.

Common birch White silvery peeling bark. Remove the feathers in autumn.

Flowering cherry The rich mahogany polished bark of this tree peels in bands to expose glossy new bark beneath. Remove lower branches in July or August, and the feathers at the same time.

Golden willow Golden yellow shoots. Once trees are two years old, cut back to 4½ft (1.4m) above ground each spring.

Scarlet willow Bright orange-scarlet young wood. Treat as golden willow.

Ornamental crab Downy bright red-purple young shoots. Remove feathers in autumn or spring.

Paperbark maple Orange-brown bark peeling to expose cinnamon-coloured young bark. Cut out suckers and remove lower branches in spring.

Snake-bark maple Jade green bark turns reddish-brown streaked silvery white. Cut out suckers and remove lower branches in spring.

Turkish hazel Grey flaking bark. Remove feathers in spring.

White-barked Himalayan birch Dazzling white/cream bark. Remove feathers in autumn.

Cavity filling **

Cavity filling can extend tree life by a number of years in situations where old or neglected trees which are otherwise healthy, develop cavities in their main branches or trunks. Ruthlessly cut out all rotten wood – right back to sound tissue. Allow to dry out before painting over all exposed wood with a safe protectant and sealant like 'Arbrex'. Then, when dry, fill in the cavity with strong mix concrete and smooth off. Finally paint over again to cover any exposed surfaces.

Container trees **

Give shelter and protection from frost and cold or drying winds.

Tender-leaved varieties of containerized trees like Japanese maple are very vulnerable to wind damage, too, as is any tree positioned in or near to draughty gaps between buildings.

55

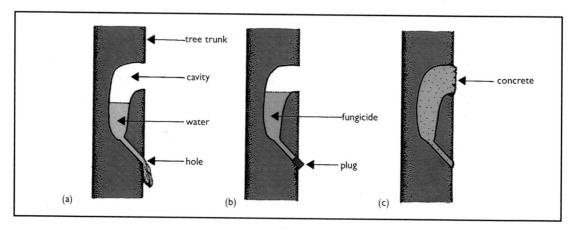

Fig 48 Cavity draining and filling: (a) Drill hole to drain out cavity;
(b) Clean out cavity plus drain and fill with liquid fungicide. Remove plug
and drain off after thirty minutes; (c) Allow cavity to dry out and then fill
the hole with concrete after treating with wood-sealing preparation.

Pest and disease control **

Spray ornamental trees where pests and diseases have already struck, or where an attack seems inevitable – invasion from a neighbour's garden perhaps? Use proprietary insecticides and fungicides. A routine spray programme should be adopted where pests and diseases are a regular occurrence.

Propagation **

Many trees can be increased from seeds sown now. Most need chilling; see page 71. Bring seeds sown earlier into the warmth to germinate. This is also the time to layer liquidambar and magnolia, and to remove and pot up, or plant out, suckers of snowy mespilus and Chusan palm. Hardwood cuttings of willow taken now should root and grow away quickly.

Care of New Trees – Extra Work

Protection **

In warm, sunny positions, and in open, windswept sites, apply proprietary anti-wilt sprays to newly planted broadleaved evergreens and conifers. Also apply them to any tree where an attempt is being made to grow under less than ideal conditions. Shade newly planted trees from strong midday sun. Fine mesh plastic netting is one of the best materials to use since it allows filtered sunlight to reach the foliage.

In hot southern gardens, wrap the trunks of thin-barked, newly planted trees, like birch and lime, with hessian strips. This is to prevent direct exposure to strong sun with a consequential risk of bark splitting.

Use animal deterrents and netting to prevent dogs urinating on the foliage of evergreens. This is especially important with low growing conifers if scorching is to be avoided. The fitting of proprietary tree guards can help in country districts to give protection against rabbits, and in towns, to prevent debarking by cats.

Harden off young trees overwintered in frames before moving outdoors.

Spraying **

Hose down the foliage of broadleaved evergreens and conifers after warm, dry or windy days.

PLANTING IN CONTAINERS

The successful cultivation of trees in containers is within the reach of almost anyone who is prepared to take time and trouble to meet somewhat exacting demands. In a word, the container tree is totally dependent upon the care of the gardener – and because the roots are restricted to a relatively small rootball, they dry out more quickly and starve sooner than similar trees grown in the ground. So, without regular attention to watering, feeding and repotting, life becomes virtually impossible. Don't forget either, when planting in containers, that it is just as important, if not more so, to match up the needs of the plants with the environment as when planting in the traditional manner anywhere else in the garden. Consider sun and shade, exposure to wind and suitability of containers and composts.

Containers

Tree containers need to meet certain basicc functional requirements while still looking attractive. When choosing a container, there are several points to keep in mind.

Looks It is not enough for the container to be of good design; it must also be compatible with the setting and blend in with its surroundings. As a general rule, quiet colours and simple designs work out the most satisfactorily. The traditional colours of black, white, stone, honey, terracotta, and pastel shades of blue and green, are a safe buy for most situations. These should merge in with most trees, as well as surrounding paving, walling and paintwork.

Size and stability It takes a great deal of compost to sustain a specimen tree with water and nutrients and provide reasonable anchorage. Think in terms of a container with a minimum depth and diameter of 14in (35cm) and up to 2ft (60cm) and more for a well-established medium to large tree. For miniature trees, don't consider troughs and sinks of under 9in (23cm) in depth. Bonsai are an exception to the general rule, and shallower containers are often used. In general, small containers need more frequent watering and feeding than large.

Regardless of size, look for stability. Reject badly proportioned, top-heavy containers. Lightweight plastics, fibreglass and wood fibre rely on the sheer weight of compost to give stability, and troubles can arise at the smaller end of the range where containers in these lightweight materials all too easily blow over.

Drainage Good drainage is essential. All out-

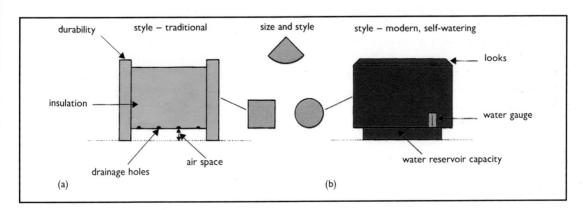

Fig 49 Container buying – points to watch. Purpose either as: (a) Pot holder; (b) Compost container.

door containers must have plenty of drainage holes in the base. This is vital where container trees are exposed to rain otherwise their roots will become waterlogged.

Durability   Trees are long lived when compared with most other garden plants. So durability, hardwearing qualities and frost resistance become the main priorities when selecting containers. Concrete and simulated stones, fibreglass and high impact plastics, along with metal, share these qualities. Earthenware pots and planters look attractive, but are liable to crack in a hard frost and will not stand up to the abuse of the inevitable odd hard knock.

Insulation   Containerized tree roots are much more vulnerable to the extremes of heat and cold than when growing in the ground – and to frost in particular. Good insulation will often make the difference between survival and death when prolonged severe weather strikes. Plastics and fibreglass give low insulation protection. Timber barrels, tubs and planters look good and have excellent insulation properties. Concrete and simulated stone will give adequate protection in all but the coldest areas where the majority of trees are going to need winter protection. See page 49. Insulation can be improved substantially by the use of liners – positioning one container inside another – but obviously this adds to cost.

Maintenance   All timber containers need painting or treating with a safe horticultural preservative to prolong their life and prevent rotting. By a similar token most metal containers need treating against rust. Another word of warning here: metal containers should be treated internally with a suitable rubberoid paint. This is to prevent the roots coming into contact with the metal with a consequential risk of poisoning. The alternative is to use metal containers with an inner liner. Plastics, fibreglass, concrete and simulated stone are all low-maintenance materials.

Shape   Box-like square planters are possibly the most popular shape, with the cylindrical type a close second. Look out, too, for half-barrels and for quarter-planters which fit neatly into corners. Choose the container shape that complements the tree as well as the setting. And bear in mind that for ease of potting and watering, the top should be as wide – or wider – than the rest of the container.

Price   Prices vary enormously and obviously depend on the size, the design and the cost of the raw materials going into the manufacture of the container. The type of container and its intended use also have a bearing on cost. Always try to relate the probable life of a container to its cost when making comparisons.

Container Composts

Since trees growing in containers need to obtain all their nutrients and moisture from a much smaller volume of soil than when growing in the ground, the rooting medium becomes of prime importance. Average garden soil is not suitable. Nor is it fertile enough to support container trees. It pans down badly, drains too slowly, holds too much water, contains too little air and there is always a risk of importing soil pests and diseases. The result? Growth is poor and inevitably roots will suffocate.

Soil-based potting composts consist of a balanced mixture of soil, peat and coarse sand, fine grit or perlite – plus fertilizer and limestone. In the case of the soilless mixtures, soil has been excluded and other ingredients are in different proportions. For average tree use, soil-based composts are preferable; they are not only easier to manage, but also retain their physical properties much longer than the soilless mixtures.

It is sound practice to buy proprietary, ready-to-use potting composts. These usually work out cheaper, are more convenient, take less work, and are a great deal safer than attempting to prepare composts at home.

One of the best known and reliable ranges of

soil-based mixtures are the John Innes composts in which most trees can be successfully grown with few problems. John Innes composts come in three strengths. J.I. No 1 is the weakest and contains a single dose of balanced fertilizer; it is used for very young trees. J.I. No 2 contains a double dose of fertilizer and is used for normal potting. J.I. No 3 is triple strength and is preferred for potting hungry or strong growing trees; it is excellent too for topdressing.

NOTE: Buy John Innes composts from a reputable firm. The quality can vary, and inferior samples do find their way on to the market.

These days, there is a swing to general-purpose soil-based composts, promoted in plenty by leading multiples and garden centres. Such composts are fine for treework, provided fertilizer levels are boosted. Mix a handful of bonemeal per bucketful of mixture when potting small trees. Double this for large trees and top-dressing.

Special mixtures: A few trees including liquidambar, magnolia, parrotia and some of the firs, grow best in lime-free composts. In these instances, seek out lime-free John Innes or similar mixtures.

Potting

Timing The ideal time to pot up trees will depend, in part at least, on the weather and the condition of the tree. Never attempt to move trees into new containers when either roots or soil are frozen, dry or saturated.

If necessary, container-grown *broadleaved, evergreen and conifer* trees can be potted at almost any time of year. The traditional planting times of spring and autumn are still best, however, when growth is at a slow ebb. These are certainly the times of year recommended for moving all evergreen trees.

Normally *deciduous* trees move with a minimum of setback in autumn, immediately after leaf fall. In any event, aim to get the job completed before the sap begins to rise in late winter and spring. This is very important when dealing with actively growing trees like birch, Japanese maple and flowering crab. If these trees are bruised or pruned just as the sap is rising, they are likely to bleed badly, and the loss of sap can be serious and weakening.

Need for potting Apart from the obvious reason of potting newly acquired trees into suitable containers, trees which are unthrifty or have grown too big for their present container are valid reasons for a move. A rough and ready rule for routine potting is to move a tree into a larger container when the height or spread of the tree exceeds three times the diameter of the container. Typical signs that repotting would be of benefit are small pale starved leaves, a rapidly drying compost (even after frequent watering), or thick roots growing out through the bottom of the container.

Preparing containers Start with clean, sound containers. New porous earthenware, concrete and simulated stone containers should all be soaked in clean water for a minimum of twenty-four hours before use. This is to remove any remaining harmful alkali, and to rehydrate the container which would otherwise rob the potting compost of moisture.

Stand large containers in their permanent positions before filling and planting. Unless they are raised up on legs, they must be stood on a level gravel bed if adequate drainage is to be ensured. Watertight drip trays should only be used in summer. Therefore, don't make the mistake of putting them under immovable heavy containers or you will risk waterlogging in winter.

With all conventional containers, large or small, it is advisable to cover the drainage holes with fine gauze or plastic mesh. With bonsai this is essential, as in the case where trees are to be plunge planted. The gauze helps to prevent worms, slugs and root-eating pests like weevils and beetles from crawling up into the container. At the same time wastage of compost washed out during watering is reduced. Once the gauze is in place, bottom out the container with a thin layer of coarse washed gravel, fine grit or clean pebbles for drainage. The choice depends on the size and depth of the container. Reserve the finest grit for small dishes and the pebbles for the largest containers. Avoid using limestone chippings for acid lovers. Cover over the drainage material with damp peat to minimize still further the wash through of compost.

Turn next to the potting compost. If it is in any way dusty and dry, moisten before use. It is easier to rewet dried-out compost before rather than after potting. Partly fill prepared containers with evenly moist potting compost.

The preparation of self-watering containers is slightly different. The potting compost must be brought into direct contact with the wicks in the base, thus cutting out the need for gauze, grit and peat.

Preparing the trees Trees will get off to a good start and become established more quickly if given care and attention before as well as after potting.

Potting creates a good opportunity to give trees a thorough inspection. Roots and branches should both be severely scrutinized.

Before attempting to remove trees from their old containers, deal with the tops. Pick over broadleaved evergreens and conifers, removing dead and decaying foliage. This prevents the spread of disease, lets in light and air, and ripens the young wood. Picking over is particularly important where varieties of thuja are grown as part of the fight against thuja blight – a disfiguring disease of the foliage. With all trees, prune out any dead or diseased wood, shortening any untidy, misplaced or straggly growths at the same time. With deciduous trees – study well, prune to shape, and thin out overcrowded branches.

Finally, take a close look for signs of pests like scale and woolly aphid. Also keep an eye open for any diseases like scab, canker and dieback, taking appropriate control measures. See page 75.

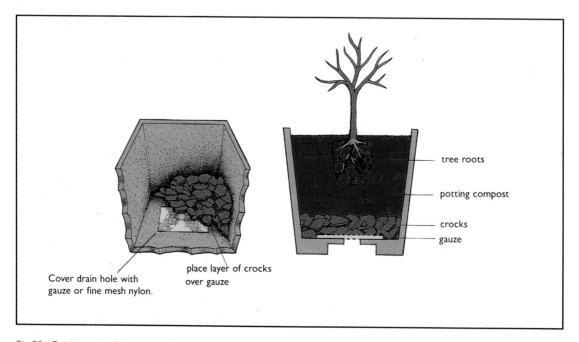

tree roots

potting compost

crocks

gauze

Cover drain hole with gauze or fine mesh nylon.

place layer of crocks over gauze

Fig 50 Potting – traditional container.

Fig 51 Amelanchier (snowy mespilus) makes an interesting small tree. Its pink young leaves turn coppery-red or scarlet in autumn. The starry-white spring flowers are followed by red fruitlets which ripen to black during the summer.

Fig 52 The humble apple tree (Malus) puts on a splendid show of spring blossom when mature – as well as providing a useful crop of fruit.

Once the top growth has been attended to, make sure the rootball is thoroughly soaked by drenching from the top until water trickles out at the bottom. Or, in the case of small containers, stand them in a bucket of clean water right up to their rims. Leave until the surface is visibly moist, then allow to drain for thirty minutes or so before disturbing the roots.

The next stage is to concentrate on the roots. Gently scrape away the loose layer of old compost from the top, taking care not to damage the surface roots. At this point the old container is removed. With small pots, place four fingers on top of the compost, then lift and invert the tree and pot with the other hand. Tap the edge of the pot sharply, two or three times, on the edge of the bench to loosen the rootball, which will then slide out of the pot with minimal damage.

Large tubs, pots and planters are very often too large to handle with ease. One practical way is to lay them gently on their sides, enlisting the help of a friend and taking care not to damage the branches. Using an old kitchen knife, ease the rootball away from the container sides. A blunt stick pushed up through the drainage holes to apply pressure from below will then force the rootball out.

With small to medium-sized trees, gently tease away and uncoil the longest roots at the bottom – and shorten them slightly. Lightly loosen the compost up the sides of the rootball before positioning the tree into a prepared container. This should be at least 2in (5cm) wider than the original. Set the top of the rootball at least 1½in (4cm) below the level of the rim, adding to or removing from the compost under the rootball as necessary. Work potting compost into the gap between rootball and container side. Firm the potting compost well as filling proceeds. Some people prefer to use a pot rammer – a dibber-like stick – but fingers will suffice. Take care with soilless composts; they should not be packed down too hard. Finally top up to within ¾in (2cm) of the rim so as to leave a space for watering.

When potting up larger trees with a rootball diameter of 10in (25cm) and over, rather more severe root pruning is required. Using a pointed stick, tease out some of the compost from around the roots in preparation for root pruning as described under repotting. Move these larger trees into tubs or planters which are at least 3in (8cm) wider than previously. Filling and firming follows a similar pattern as for the smaller trees, except that the top of the compost is left about 1in (3cm) below the rim so as to hold more water.

When potting up seedlings or transplants, with no pot size for guidance, settle for a container with a diameter of not less than half the spread. Or, in the case of tall, but narrow, trees – with a diameter of not less than half the height. Set the trees at the same depth as before the move, and again allow space for watering.

Repotting

Once trees have reached the maximum height accepted as being in keeping with their setting, keep them healthy, without getting appreciably larger, by repotting and topdressing. Repotting is carried out in much the same way as potting on, but trees are returned to containers of the same size instead of a larger one. Having removed the tree from its container, reduce the rootball size by root pruning, taking the width and depth down by a quarter. Avoid rough handling of the roots. After teasing away the old compost with a pointed stick, cut away old exposed roots with pruners.

Topdressing

With medium-sized and large container trees it is neither normal nor necessary to pot every year. It is adequate to topdress in alternate years or even in two years out of three.

Pull out the weeds and remove any moss before carefully scraping away the top ½–1½in (1–4cm) of old compost – without inflicting damage to the roots. Top up with fresh compost to within ½–¾in (1–2cm) of the rim. If much of the surface compost has already been washed away, leaving exposed roots, just remove weeds and moss; then prick to loosen and roughen the surface crust, using a pointed stick. Then fill up with fresh compost. Never try to 'dig-out' compost or the roots are likely to be damaged.

Plunge Planting

On occasions, trees could be of benefit in situations where it is unwise to plant up in the traditional manner. Perhaps their roots would be a nuisance or tree size needs to be restricted; maybe the soil is unsuitable; possibly a temporary display is needed for a special occasion; perhaps the garden is about to undergo alterations; or, in the case of planting dwarf trees into sink gardens and windowboxes, future potting is made much easier. One answer to all these problems is to plant out pot-grown trees, complete with container, which is plunged up to its rim.

Whether in sink garden or windowbox, bed or border, rock garden or focal point – planting schemes can be altered instantly. Trees are easily lifted, complete with pot, and removed elsewhere without setback. All plunge-planted trees need regular watering in dry weather. They also need potting on or repotting – small specimens once a year, medium to large in alternate years.

Immediate Aftercare and Management

Support   Immediately after potting make sure that trees are securely staked and tied.

Watering   As soon as potting and staking are completed, water all trees throughly to settle the soil around the roots. To minimize the washing away of compost from around the roots, use a can with a fine rose.

After the initial watering, try to delay watering

Fig 53   Plunge planting. When plunge planting set out the tree complete with original container sunk up to the rim.

FLOWERING TREES

Broadleaved trees		
Amelanchier lamarckii	Snowy Mespilus	Sp
Arbutus unedo	Strawberry Tree	Au-Win
Cercis siliquastrum	Judas Tree	Sp
Cornus mas	Cornelian Cherry	Win-Sp
Cotoneaster × 'Hybridus Pendulus'	Weeping Cotoneaster	Su
Crataegus prunifolia	Plum-leaf Thorn	Sp-Su
Cytisus battandierii	Moroccan Broom	Sp-Su
Davidia involucrata	Handkerchief Tree	Sp
Eucalyptus niphophila	Snow Gum	Su
Koelreuteria paniculata 'Fastigiata'	Golden Rain Tree	Su
Laburnum × watereri 'Vossii'	Laburnum	Su
Magnolia × soulangiana	Magnolia	Sp
Malus	Apple	Sp
Malus 'John Downie'	Flowering Crab	Sp
Malus 'Profusion'	Purple-leaved Flowering Crab	Sp
Parrotia persica	Parrotia	Sp
Prunus 'Pendula Rosea'	Weeping Cherry	Sp
Prunus persica	Flowering Peach	Sp
Prunus 'Pissardii'	Purple-leaf Plum	Sp
Pyrus salicifolia 'Pendula'	Weeping Silver Pear	Sp
Rhus typhina	Stag's Horn Sumach	Su
Robinia pseudoacacia	False Acacia	Su
Salix caprea 'Kilmarnock'	Kilmarnock Willow	Sp
Sophora tetraptera 'Grandiflora'	Pagoda Tree	Sp
Sorbus aria 'Lutescens'	Whitebeam	Sp-Su
Sorbus aucuparia	Mountain Ash	Sp-Su
Syringa vulgaris	Lilac	Sp-Su
Tamarix gallica	Tamarisk	Su

Sp=Spring   Su=Summer   Au=Autumn   Win=Winter

again for seven to ten days – to encourage a vigorous root action. But don't let the roots or compost dry out.

Mist over newly potted trees every day. This is especially important with bonsai. Thereafter, once they are growing away freely, moisten during the evening after warm, dry or windy days.

Shade Protect newly potted trees from direct strong sun, using lath or fine mesh netting screens. At midday cover with muslin or coloured plastic netting.

Wind After dryness, wind is one of the worst hazards to newly planted container trees. Ideally, encircle groups of trees with fine mesh netting, fixed to a high support, until established. If wind or dryness seem a likely hazard, don't neglect to spray the foliage of newly potted trees with an anti-wilt preparation. See page 56.

CHAPTER 6

Pruning and Training

THE PURPOSE OF PRUNING

While most people readily accept the need to prune and train shrubs and edible fruit trees, there are those who question the necessity when it comes to decorative trees. It is true that many trees do grow satisfactorily with little or no regular pruning or detailed training. But there are many more which are greatly improved by careful attention to these two basic operations. Indeed, in certain instances, pruning and training are essential.

There are a number of very sound reasons for pruning and training.

1. To enhance the appearance of the tree. Pruning improves the quality of flowers, fruit and foliage.
2. To keep trees to the shape and form intended.

Fig 54 Laburnum. *Pruning improves the quality of flowers, fruit and foliage.*

3. To control tree vigour and growth – interlinked with productivity. All these factors can be regulated according to the severity of pruning. For instance, hard cutting of deciduous varieties in autumn or spring results in vigorous growth, even though it is very often at the expense of prolific flowering and heavy fruiting. On the credit side the quality and size of the flowers and fruit are invariably improved. Light pruning, on the other hand, brings about diminished growth and, in the short term at least, an increase in flower production can be expected.
4. To extend the useful productive life of the tree. By cutting out old and tired wood, the development of a steady succession of new replacement shoots is encouraged – to carry flowers, fruit and foliage.
5. Finally, to maintain trees in a healthy and safe condition. The removal of dead wood minimizes the risk of disease as well as of falling branches.

NOTE: By timely attention to pruning and training, the shape of many trees can be manipulated, in part at least, to suit the situation. Bush and standard forms illustrate this point well, as do intensive and wall-trained trees. Cordons, espaliers and fans are all the result of specialist pruning and training, and without it wall-trained trees would not have become a commercial reality.

PRUNING TOOLS AND EQUIPMENT

Don't rush out and buy a whole range of tools for pruning. Stop and weigh up exactly what is essential. This avoids the financial embarrassment of buying a whole range of expensive equipment which may never be needed, and cuts down on the demands for valuable storage space. In a modern garden, where one or two trees are the norm, a pair of hand pruners, a strong, sharp knife and a small pruning saw will usually suffice. Where trees have grown to an appreciable height, a long arm pruner and some steps will probably be called for. Think very carefully before buying such tools as power saws and shredders; they involve a considerable outlay for very limited use. It usually makes better sense to hire such items. Rates are very reasonable.

It is important when buying any piece of equipment to make sure it is of a suitable weight and size for the individual concerned. Not only is the work less tiring, but fewer accidents are likely.

BASIC PRUNING

Before starting to prune, ensure all cutting tools are clean and sharp.

Making a cut Generally speaking, always cut cleanly back to a healthy, plump bud. Avoid tearing the bark or leaving a jagged, 'chewed' finish. Aim to make a gently sloping downward cut, starting about ⅛in (3mm) above the bud. The cut should slope away from the bud to reduce the risk of directing water towards the bud to set up rots.

Saw cuts Don't make bigger or more cuts than necessary. All saw cuts should be smoothed off with a sharp knife.

Painting Always protect pruning cuts of ¾in (2cm) and over by painting immediately with a proprietary pruning sealant.

Removing snags Avoid leaving 'snags'. These are short, blind stubs of stem devoid of a good bud or shoot. They not only look untidy, but provide entry points for disease as they inevitably die back. Cut back flush to avoid problems.

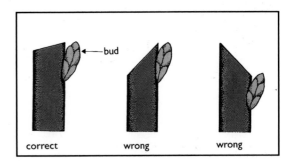

Fig 55 Pruning cuts.

Lopping The basis of much tree surgery involves the removal or shortening back of branches as the dead, unsound or diseased wood is cut back to sound tissue.

Take great care not to split the portion of the branch/trunk which is to remain. This is to minimize the risk of diseases gaining entry to start off rots within the wood. Splitting can normally be avoided by cutting off a manageable section at a time. Always undercut the limb about one-third through, before cutting downwards from above. Finally, the redundant limb should be sawn through flush with the main trunk or branch so as not to leave a snag.

Don't attempt to carry out lopping while the wood is frosted. Splitting is difficult to avoid under these conditions.

Prunings Never leave prunings lying around. Gather up and burn, or cart to the nearest tip.

Safety When young children are around, avoid using pruning tools — and always store them in safety out of harm's way.

PRUNING AND TRAINING TECHNIQUES

The choice of method and time of pruning or training must be related to the variety, age and condition of the tree. In addition, the purpose which the tree is to serve needs to be taken into account. Also, as will become apparent in the

65

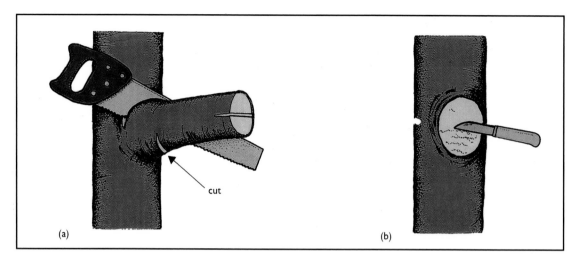

(a)

cut

(b)

Fig 56   Lopping and limb removal: (a) Shorten heavy limbs in sections. Finally undercut about a third of the way through before cutting down flush with the trunk. (b) Smooth off the rough saw cuts with a knife and afterwards paint the wound with a safe protectant.

following pages, wall-trained trees are treated somewhat differently to free-standing forms, even when of the same variety.

Variety

Please refer to individual tree entries for any detailed modifications before starting to prune. See Chapter 9.

Young Trees – General

In practice, before being offered for sale, most garden trees are partly trained with their basic framework of branches already formed. Pruning thereafter is an ongoing process which, as far as the average gardener is concerned, normally begins at planting time.

Being of a naturally neat habit, broadleaved evergreen and conifer container-raised trees usually need a minimum of initial top pruning. Simply shorten back straggly, misplaced or damaged shoots. Avoid any hard cutting back into old leafless wood, especially on conifers – you will risk exposing bare stems to view as a permanent feature.

Deciduous trees are much more variable in their needs. As with evergreens, ornamentals raised in containers need little pruning other than shaping the crown by shortening overlong straggly shoots. Again, it is important to cut back damaged shoots.

Weeping trees are treated in a similar manner to their evergreen or deciduous counterparts.

Root trimming

At planting time shorten back any damaged or overlong roots to sound tissue, but keep cutting to a minimum.

Young Trees – Formation Pruning

Essentially, formation pruning is all about the treatment needed to form a main basic framework of branches on deciduous trees. It is rarely necessary where nursery trained trees are bought in. Sometimes, however, it is possible to get hold of young maiden whips. Since substantial savings can be made by home training, some enthusiasts are tempted to try their hand. The following notes are for their benefit.

Bush and standard trees

Starting with a single-stem, unbranched maiden whip of a decorative deciduous tree, proceed as follows.

In autumn, cut back the main stem to a good bud about 6in (15cm) above the anticipated height of clear trunk. Where, for example, the aim is to form a bush tree with an 18in (45cm) clear trunk between soil level and bottom branch, cut back the whip to about 2ft (60cm) above ground. By a similar token, to grow a standard tree with a 6ft (1.8m) clear trunk, prune to a bud about 6½ft (1.95m) above ground level.

As a result of this initial pruning, three to five strong shoots should develop and be ready for pruning in autumn – a year after cutting back. Shorten these new growths by one-third to a half, and aim to create a bowl-shaped framework of main branches above a clear trunk. Remove any surplus shoots from the trunk as they arise.

Within a year, additional shoots will break away, and normal routine pruning can begin.

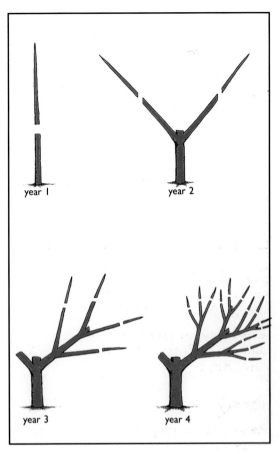

Fig 58 Formation pruning – fan.

Fig 57 Formation pruning – bush tree. Cut out ingrowing, downward and crossing branches as well as the weak and misplaced shoots. Aim to achieve an open-centred, bowl-shaped framework of branches.

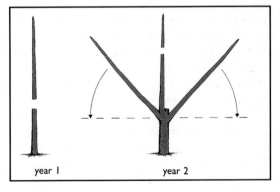

Fig 59 Formation pruning – escalier. In year 2, leave the left and right limbs uncut, but bend down to horizontal and tie.

Routine Pruning

It is dangerous to generalize. The actual technique for, and time of, routine pruning must be related to the individual variety, its habit, its training and its use.

Free-standing broadleaved, evergreens and conifers – including weeping varieties

When grown as free-standing natural forms most evergreens, including conifers, need little or no pruning, especially in their early years.

Evergreens are normally pruned during the warmer months from May to August. Avoid

Fig 60   The stiffly weeping habit of Salix caprea 'Kilmarnock' can be gauged from this catkin-covered young tree.

cutting them, unless absolutely necessary, during hard weather and in freezing conditions.

Cut out dead and dying branches. Shorten back straggly, untidy and misplaced shoots. Remove any badly scorched foliage, but avoid cutting into old wood. This is most important with conifers. Many varieties are reluctant to break away and produce new foliage on old stems.

It is not uncommon for single stem trees to develop a forked head. Cut out the weakest or most poorly positioned stem, leaving only the strongest, best placed leader.

Hedges and screens

The aim when dealing with tree hedges and screens should be to provide and maintain fairly dense, close-knit foliage and branches. The methods used need to be modified to suit the type of screen required – formal or semi-formal.

In order to obtain and maintain top-to-toe foliage, without bare stems and gaps at the base, keep all hedges and screens wider at the bottom than at the top.

Free-standing deciduous trees including weeping varieties

Bush, standard and multi-stem trees are best pruned in autumn about leaf fall. Notable exceptions to the rule are trees grown intensively or formally. These are summer pruned to restrain. Crab apple responds well to this treatment. The popular flowering cherry, plum, almond and peach present other exceptions to the autumn pruning generalization. Aim to prune these about July or August when the risk of silver leaf infection is least.

If the opportunity to prune in autumn is missed, don't worry unduly. The vast majority of deciduous trees are fine pruned in spring. However, never prune walnut, birch, maple or poplar in spring. They bleed badly and this weakens them drastically. Stunted growth is likely, and all too often disease gets a hold.

Cut out dead, diseased and ingrowing stems and branches. Shorten misplaced, weakly, straggly or crossing shoots.

In the case of single centre-stem trees where there is evidence of forking, remove the weakest or worst placed of the forked shoots as with evergreens.

Wall-trained decorative trees

The routine pruning of wall-trained decorative trees is quite straightforward – once the initial branch framework has been formed. This is usually in the form of espalier or fan. Prune according to the tree's natural habit.

Some trees like laburnum, *Cytisus battandieri* (Moroccan broom) and crab apple, flower on short spurs on three-year-old wood and older. In this case carry out summer pruning in July and August. Shorten back each new season's growth to about three buds. Then in September-October, shorten secondary late growths back to one bud. Where flowering spurs become large and clumsy, thin these out in autumn. But leave at least a couple of buds per spur. These will break away and form future flowering wood.

Other trees like peach, flower mainly on young wood. These are treated as described for fruiting peach and nectarine.

A few trees like magnolia, flower mainly on old wood. They are naturally fairly tidy and need little more than the occasional light pruning to retain tree shape.

Remedial Pruning

Non-flowering and excess vigour

This is a problem which can often be improved by root pruning. Both evergreen and deciduous varieties are best root pruned in autumn while the soil is still likely to be warm and moist.

Dig a semi-circular trench about 2–2½ft (60–75cm) out from the trunk. Make it at least 12in (30cm) wide and deep. Cut through any thick roots crossing the trench as digging pro-

Fig 61   Malus 'John Downie' has attractive fruit. They are first class for making jelly.

ceeds. Take care to damage the delicate fibrous roots as little as possible. Backfill the trench with good topsoil, working it in and firming it around the fibrous roots. Dig out a second semi-circular trench on the other side of the tree, so as to encircle the tree completely. After backfilling, water thoroughly to settle the soil. In exposed gardens, stake and tie securely.

Wrongly sited trees

It is sometimes possible to move an established tree to a new position, provided it is not too big to handle or too old to move. Any tree planted within the last two or three years should move with few problems. See page 28.

Trees which are too high

This is a fairly common problem. It is often practical to drop the height of a tree by a quarter to a third, but no more. Use the method commonly known as 'heading out' or 'heading back'.

Carry out the work during summer when dealing with evergreens, but delay until autumn for deciduous trees.

With narrow, columnar, single centre-stem trees the idea is to cut out the top portion of the tree, making the saw cut as inconspicuous as possible. This is relatively easy, in theory at least, with trees which have upswept branches. Make the saw cut below the level of the branch tips.

In confined spaces, or where the centre trunk is obviously heavy, it is safer to remove small sections at a time. And if there is any risk of damage from falling timber, lashing with rope is advisable. Tie one end of a sound rope securely to the portion about to be cut off. Incidentally, the rope needs to be long enough to reach the ground and still have enough length left to enable it to be looped round the tree. Allowing sufficient slack to enable sawing to take place unimpeded, wind the rope twice round the main trunk, then over a branch to prevent downward slippage. Hold the rope taut and tie the free end to another branch lower down. Saw off the section; it will only fall as far as the slack of the rope permits. Untie the rope and gently lower the section to the ground.

Wide-spreading trees

To reduce the size of trees which have several main branches of similar thickness, shorten back the tips of each main branch. Commonly referred to as 'crown reduction' or 'de-horning', this is a technique used to deal with many deciduous trees. Very few evergreens will comfortably survive the treatment, holly being the one exception. Conifers don't take kindly to it. As a rule bare, often ugly, limbs are left behind.

The work is normally best carried out in late summer or early autumn. Never remove more than one-third of a branch or there is a risk of dying back. And always ensure that the head is narrower at the top than at the sides.

When it comes to the problem of excessive ground shade and overcrowding, it is unfortunately very often the spreading evergreens and conifers which are at fault – the very trees which are intolerant of 'de-horning'. Here 'crown-lifting' can help. This involves the removal of some of the branches. Start at the bottom and work upwards, so increasing the height of headroom under the tree.

Dense-headed trees

Only a few garden trees suffer from this problem. Sometimes, deciduous varieties – notably crab apple and thorn – make excessively dense heads which need fairly drastic 'crown thinning'.

Crown thinning is usually best carried out immediately after leaf fall. The branches are more clearly visible at this time. First, cut out all the thin, weak, spindly and ingrowing branches. Then, if the centre of the crown is still very overcrowded, selectively cut out a few more branches to create an open centre bowl arrangement.

Unsound or unsafe trees

Many an old or part-rotten tree can be saved and given a new lease of life by tree surgery. Where large or very high trees are involved, it is usually best to leave the work to a qualified and trained tree surgeon.

Cankers

One job which should never be neglected is the prompt removal of cankers. Bare, circular or oval patches, surrounded by raised, roughened bark – with sunken and rotting centres – are characteristic symptoms of cankers.

Where a branch is completely encircled with these bare patches, there is no alternative but to remove the affected branch.

In the case of small cankers, cut out affected areas, and smooth over with a sharp knife. Immediately paint over all wounds with a proprietary anti-canker compound.

CHAPTER 7

Propagation

The busy average gardener, impatient for quick results, is probably well advised to rely on buying part-grown, ready to plant young trees. But if there is no hurry to plant up for a few years, or the intention is to grow bonsai, then there is some merit in raising trees. This is particularly true in the case of bonsai, since training can then start at a very early age, offering a distinct advantage.

There is a lot of satisfaction to be gained in propagating trees. However, be prepared to pay attention to detail — and to wait anything from three to five years and longer before they are large enough to set out in their final positions in the garden.

PROPAGATION METHODS

Many tree varieties can be raised from seed, but not all. Some don't grow true to type. One advantage of starting from seed is the ready availability of seed, when compared with, say, acquiring grafting material. Another bonus is the relative ease with which the job is carried out. The minimal cost, too, is an attraction. On the debit side, however, seed tends to take longer than any other method of propagation, and there is usually some variation among plants.

Other methods of tree propagation range from the easy suckers, cuttings and layers, to the more demanding budding and grafting. Most trees are suited more to one technique than another. See individual tree entries in Chapter 9.

Trees which are increased by methods other than seed normally share identical characteristics with their parent plants. Good features as well as

bad are passed on from one generation to the next. So always propagate from the very best trees, making sure they possess sought-after good characteristics. Another point to watch is that any tree being used as a parent should be free from virus and other diseases which can be passed on in the sap. Avoid propagating from any tree which looks unhealthy, perhaps with distorted leaves and shoots or showing uncharacteristic leaf mottling or discoloration.

Growing from Seed

Always aim to use fresh seed, harvested within twelve months prior to sowing. Reputable seed houses date-stamp their packets. Store seed in cool, dry conditions out of the reach of vermin until required for sowing. Try to start off seeds at a time when conditions are most likely to favour germination and subsequent early growth. The seed of many trees is best sown between December and mid-February.

Pre-treatment The vast majority of tree seed requires pre-sowing treatment of some sort to improve and hasten germination. Most seeds benefit from a soaking in tepid — not hot — water for eight to twelve hours. After soaking, the likes of apple, pear and eucalyptus are sown right away. But many others such as conifers, cotoneaster, mountain ash and whitebeam require a subsequent period of chilling to break seed dormancy. Simply mix the moistened seed with damp peat and put it into a clean plastic bag. Then store in a refrigerator for three to eight weeks before sowing. The alternative, and in some ways preferable, method is to sow immediately after soaking and chill the seed as part of the post-sowing operation.

Seed sowing Use small pots or trays with a minimum depth of 3in (8cm). Cover the bottom with the fine gravel before filling to within about ½in (lcm) of the rim with a good proprietary seed compost. Sow small seeds like birch and some of the conifers by scattering thinly on the surface, then barely covering with more fine compost. With larger seeds and pips, cover the seed to a depth equal to the diameter of the seed and no more. Similar guidelines apply to stones, but these are usually popped into dibber holes and covered.

Germination Water the sown containers from below by standing to half their depth in water. Remove immediately the surface is visibly moist and allow to drain for about twenty minutes before covering with clear plastic sheet or cling film. Seeds which require no special after-treatment are kept as a comfortable room temperature of about 60°F (16°C) to germinate. Where chilling is carried out after sowing, in preference to before, stand the containers outdoors in a safe spot, sheltered from rain. Make sure the seeds are protected from birds and vermin. After six to eight weeks of chilling, move the containers into the warmth to germinate.

Keep the seeds warm, moist and shaded from strong sun. Remove the plastic covering at the first sign of movement; this is usually within four to eight weeks. Some tree seeds will not germinate during the first year. This is because they suffer from a condition known as 'double dormancy', and they need a second spell of chilling. So if seeds do fail to germinate promptly, don't throw them out for up to eighteen months at least – and don't allow them to dry out during this period.

Pricking out and potting As soon as seedlings are big enought to handle, prick them out singly into small pots of weak potting compost. Keep them watered and stand outdoors in mild, warm weather. Overwinter under cover. Pot on young trees into progressively larger containers until they are ready to transplant into their final positions.

Growing from Suckers

Trees which have the suckering habit include lilac, Chusan palm and stag's horn sumach. Provided there is access to rooted suckers, they are increased simply and easily. Carefully dig out sturdy suckers with as much root as possible. The ideal time is during autumn, when growth is at a low ebb. The rooted suckers are potted up or planted out into well-prepared soil in a sheltered spot. Either way they need to be grown on for a year or two before setting out in the garden.

NOTE: It is important to establish whether suckers arise from what was originally a rootstock. If this proves to be the case they will subsequently need to be budded or grafted with a recognized garden variety.

Growing from Layers

The pegging down of layers is a relatively safe, easy and inexpensive way to propagate trees. Provided that some young and healthy shoots are within reach of the ground, layering is possible with many trees. The best times to carry out the work are during autumn and spring.

Select a strong one- or two-year-old shoot. Some 12in (30cm) in from the tip, remove the leaves to expose a 6in (15cm) length of clear stem. Next take a sharp knife and make a slanting cut about half-way through the stem from the underside – at the point where the leaves were removed. Pull down the stem and mark the spot where the cut meets the ground. Scoop out a shallow hollow and pin the stem down into it. A wooden peg or length of stiff wire serves the purpose well. Bend the stem up at the point it is pegged and tie the tip of the layer to a short bamboo cane pushed firmly into the ground.

Finally, pack around the wounded area of the stem with weak potting compost.

Keep the soil moist around the layer. As soon as it is well rooted (it usually takes one or two years), sever it from the parent tree. Lift and plant out either in autumn or spring.

Growing from Cuttings

Cuttings are a useful way to increase certain deciduous, evergreen and conifer trees. Although there are several different ways of taking, preparing and treating cuttings, in practice there are two main techniques with only minor variations.

Hardwood cuttings Are so called because they are prepared from ripened and lignified or hardened wood of the new season's growths.

These are normally taken in autumn after leaf fall, being eminently suitable for deciduous trees. Select well-ripened, pencil-thick shoots, about 12–16in (30–40cm) in length. This allows for trimming. A prepared cutting of 8–12in (20–30cm) is somewhere near the ideal.

Trim the bottom of the cutting squarely just below a leaf joint (node), using a sharp pair of pruners. Then cut off the soft tip, about ⅛in (3mm) above a bud and back into ripe wood. Dip the bottom end of the cutting into a proprietary rooting preparation, before inserting into previously prepared soil in a garden frame or sheltered spot outdoors. Make dibber holes about 6in (15cm) deep and a similar distance apart. Trickle a little sand into each hole before positioning a cutting. Firm the soil around the cuttings and water in if the ground seems dry. Keep them well watered and weed-free until

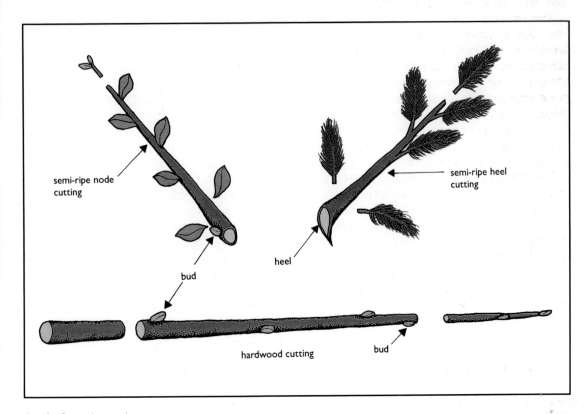

semi-ripe node cutting

semi-ripe heel cutting

heel

bud

bud

hardwood cutting

Fig 62 Preparing cuttings.

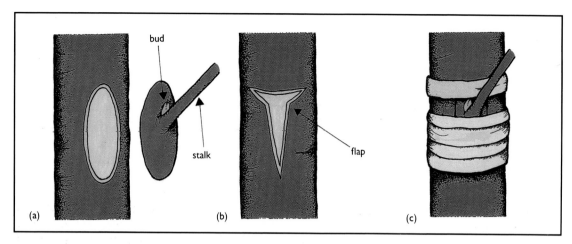

Fig 63 Budding: (a) Remove a sliver of bark with the scion bud and cut off the leaf, leaving a short stalk; (b) Make a matching 'T' cut in the rootstock and slide the bud behind the flaps of bark; (c) Bind the stem with grafting tape to hold the bud in place and prevent drying out.

rooted and ready to move. This is normally by the following autumn. If hardwood cuttings are rooted under a frame, ventilate freely on mild days until spring, when the lights are left off altogether.

Semi-hardwood cuttings Are the main alternative to hardwood, and are used for both evergreen and deciduous varieties. Cuttings are prepared from firm, half-ripe new wood. They are normally taken during summer or early autumn before the shoots become hard and brittle. In the cool of the day select firm, healthy growths about 6–8in (15–20cm) in length. Avoid taking wilted cuttings at all costs – if necessary give copious amounts of water to the tree the day before.

Prepare the cuttings by shortening to just below the bottom leaf joint, cutting the stem cleanly and squarely. Remove the soft tip back to just above a bud, leaving a cutting of about 4–6in (10–15cm) in length. Finally, pull off the lower leaves to expose about one-third of the stem.

A higher success rate is sometimes possible by removing sideshoots with a heel – a piece of older wood attached at the base. Heel cuttings are taken by pulling a sideshoot downwards and away from the stem. Don't use a knife or pruners at this stage. Neaten the tail of bark at the bottom of the cutting by shortening with a knife.

Remove the tip and lower leaves as described for traditional semi-hardwood cuttings.

Dip the bottom of all cuttings into proprietary rooting preparation. Insert three or four prepared cuttings around the edge of a 4in (10cm) pot, or set them singly into 3in (8cm) pots, of cutting compost. Firm lightly. A mixture of equal parts by bulk of moss peat and coarse sand or fine grit makes an excellent rooting medium.

Water the cuttings in and root them in shade – under a frame, in a greenhouse or indoors. Keep them humid and warm. Where the atmosphere is likely to be dry, encase each pot in a perforated clear plastic bag to maintain humidity. Alternatively, place in a propagator. Some varieties root better in a heated propagator – see individual tree entries in Chapter 9. When rooted, remove the covering and pot up singly into small pots of soil-based potting compost. Overwinter under a frame or indoors. Grow on for two, three or more years until ready to plant out, potting on into larger containers as necessary.

Budding and Grafting

Space does not permit more than a mention of these methods. Readers wishing to learn more about budding and grafting are advised to consult a specialist manual.

CHAPTER 8

Tree Problems

Growing any tree in an unfavourable environment can cause many problems. Neglect and
faulty feeding, watering and pruning further compound troubles, with weak or sickly trees as the
result. Such trees are likely to need a lot more
nursing along than when given reasonable growing conditions. They are also likely to succumb
when put under stress from pests and diseases.

Prevention is better than cure. Good cultivations and timely attention to detail provide the
key to success. A healthy tree is better able to
resist disease and will stand a good chance of
shaking off pest attacks.

Pests

Aphids

Symptoms Distorted, twisted and puckered
leaves with colonies of greenish, bluish or black
insects congregating at and around the growing
points. In bad attacks leaves and shoots become
covered with honeydew – a shiny sticky secretion
on which soot-like black moulds often grow.
Aphids are sap-sucking insects and carriers of
virus diseases.

Treatment Spray affected trees with insecticide
at the first signs of trouble. Give tar oil winter
wash to deciduous trees following severe attacks,
to destroy the eggs.

Birds

Symptoms Pecked and eaten ripening fruits.
Bud loss in winter – cherry, peach, plum and nectarine are particularly vulnerable. Bullfinches are
notorious for bud stripping.

Treatment Where practical, net fruit trees in a
cage. Those trained against a wall are most at
risk, being more exposed and more readily seen.
Use bird scarers where the use of netting is not
possible.

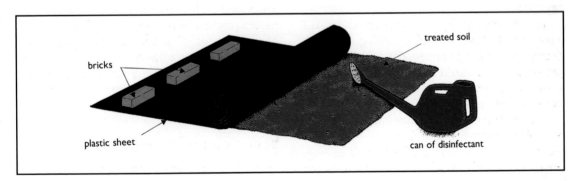

Fig 64 *Soil disinfection. Water the affected area with disinfectant. Cover
with plastic sheeting to keep in the fumes. Lay bricks on the sheet to
keep it in place.*

Common green capsid bug (Lygus pabulinus)

Symptoms Tiny brown spots on the leaves are often accompanied by small brown-edged holes, and distortion on young leaves. Fruits are malformed and disfigured, especially on apple and pear. The winged adults are flattish, green and roughly oval, about ¼in (6mm) long. Both the adults and the wingless, colourless, grub-like nymphs feed on the sap.

Treatment: As for aphids.

Caterpillars

Symptoms Leaves, buds, flowers, shoots and fruits eaten and holed. Usually the caterpillars are to be found close by. These are the young grubs of many kinds of moth and butterfly, and come in many colours including greens, browns and multicolours. Some are hairy. In severe attacks trees can be defoliated.

Treatment In the case of small-scale attacks on young trees, handpick the caterpillars and destroy them. Otherwise, spray with insecticide during the growing season; and apply tar oil winter wash to dormant deciduous trees.

Red spider mites (Panonychus ulmi)

Symptoms Mottled and yellowing leaves. Minute, almost too small to see with the naked eye, red or yellowish-red insects mass in large numbers on the leaf undersides. In bad attacks fine spider-like webbing becomes discernible. Leaf bronzing and premature defoliation and stunted growth may well result. Attacks are normally worse in prolonged dry weather. Red spider mites are sap feeders.

Treatment Hose newly planted and young trees with water in the evenings during warm, dry, windy weather and following hot days. This will discourage the pest while freshening up the foliage. Apply insecticide sprays at 14 to 21-day intervals during the growing season. The exception is fruit trees – don't spray while crops are ripening. Spray dormant deciduous trees with tar oil winter wash to kill off overwintering eggs.

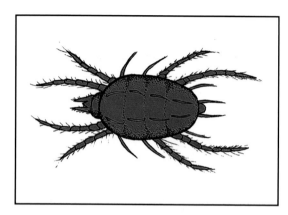

Fig 65 Red spider mite.

Woolly aphid (Eriosoma lanigerum)

Symptoms Conspicuous patches of whitish cottonwool-like waxy covering appear on the bark and trunk of affected trees. When removed, colonies of brownish or purplish insects are revealed. In bad attacks trees can become stunted and weakened. Apple, pear, cotoneaster and thorn are among those most at risk.

Treatment Where they are reachable, paint affected patches with methylated spirits throughout the growing season. Cut out any badly affected spurs on wall-trained fruits which are very often the worst hit. Apply a tar oil winter spray to pest-infested deciduous trees.

Diseases

Canker (various)

Symptoms See page 70. There are several canker-causing disease organisms, and all usually gain entry through pruning wounds and stubs, insect injury, or diseased tissue. Trees most at risk include apple, peach, plum, cherry and poplar.

Treatment   See page 70.

Coral spot (Nectria cinnabarina)

Symptoms   Pink pustules, reminiscent of tiny pin-cushions, arise on dead wood, typically where shoots have died or where pruning stubs were left to die back. This fungus disease enters by attacking dead tissue. It then spreads to living wood.

Treatment   Cut out and dispose of diseased shoots and branches. Paint over all wounds with a sealant. Apply tar oil winter spray to dormant deciduous trees.

Damping off (Pythium, phytophthora and Rhizcotonia spp)

Symptoms   Typically seedlings rot off at soil level fall over and die – this is due to infection by any one of several plant disease organisms.

Treatment   Always sow seeds in clean containers and use fresh sowing compost. Ideally, water in or dust seeds with fungicide at, or immediately after, sowing. Avoid overwatering. Avoid stagnant, cold or very warm conditions – both favour damping off. Prevention, coupled with good management, is the only satisfactory answer. There is no cure.

Fireblight (Erwinia amylovora)

Symptoms   Affected foliage, flowers, shoots and even whole branches become withered, blackened and die. Trees at risk include apple, pear, crab, cotoneaster, thorn and whitebeam.

Treatment   Cut back all withered shoots and branches to sound wood. Then remove all diseased prunings. Avoid replanting with susceptible varieties in areas where fireblight is prevalent.

Honey fungus (Armillaria mellea)

Symptoms   Affected trees progressively wilt and eventually die. Expect honey-coloured toadstools to appear at or near soil level. The fungus spreads mainly by means of underground rhizomorphs – black or brown bootlace-like strands which travel out from affected trees. Most trees are at risk.

Treatment   Dig out and remove from site any affected trees. Take care to dig out all the rhizomorphs. Drench the surrounding soil with a cresylic acid disinfectant immediately to try to contain the fungus.

Mildews (various)

Symptoms   Leaves and tips of new shoots, as well as buds, flowers and older leaves, become covered with whitish meal-like dust. This weakens and disfigures the tree. Apple, crab and thorn are liable to attack.

Treatment   Cut out and dispose of badly affected shoots. Apply a good fungicide spray at the first signs of attack. Repeat at 21-day intervals during the growing season. Stop spraying edible crops before the fruits start to ripen – don't start again until after harvesting.

Peach leaf curl (Taphrina deformans)

Symptoms   Puckered and deformed leaves are red at first and become white later. Premature leaf fall is typical. Trees are weakened. Almond, peach and nectarines are frequently attacked.

Treatment   Apply spring and autumn sprays of fungicide, before leaf opening and after leaf fall.

Rusts (various)

Symptoms   Yellow or orange pustules on leaf undersides are typical. Tree foliage is discoloured and the appearance is spoilt. Various trees occasionally come under attack.

Treatment Not as a rule necessary. But in severe cases apply a fungicide spray.

Scab (Venturia)

Symptoms Characteristic black spots on fruits and leaves and premature leaf drop. If left unchecked, flowering and fruiting may suffer. Apple, crab and pear are vulnerable to infection.

Treatment Where scab was suspected in the previous year apply fungicide sprays at intervals. Start when green flower buds show, spray when buds show pink, and again at petal fall.

Silver leaf (Stereum purpureum)

Symptoms Silvering of leaves, followed by purplish fungal outgrowths on dead or dying branches, are typical. Infected trees are often killed. Plum, peach, nectarine, apple, apricot and cherry are all at risk.

Treatment Cut back and dispose of branches with silvered foliage. Continue to cut back until the wood is completely clear of brown staining. As a preventive measure carry out any pruning of plums and cherries between June and August — wounds heal naturally at this time and trees are less vulnerable to infection.

Disorders

Browning or dying foliage

Possible causes Excessive dryness at the roots. Strong sun, wind and frost. Root damage due to injury or waterlogging.

Treatment Apply anti-wilt spray to newly planted conifers. Syringe the foliage of all newly planted trees, particularly after hot days and during dry windy weather. Keep them well watered.

Bud, flower and fruitlet drop

Possible causes Root dryness, shallow soil, root injury and over-production of buds and flowers.

Treatment Keep roots moist. Don't neglect mulching. Protect roots from injury, pest, diseases and competition from weeds, grass and nearby plants. When planting trees make sure the ground is well prepared.

Chlorosis

Possible causes Attempting to grow lime-hating trees on soil with high levels of lime or chalk, or watering lime-haters in containers with hard water.

Treatment Avoid planting lime-haters like parrotia and katsura trees on chalky soil — rather grow them in containers of lime-free compost. Use rainwater for watering container trees in hard-water areas rather than the mains supply. It is uneconomic to treat any but the youngest and smallest of trees with iron sequestrene, the control for chlorosis.

Failure to set fruit

Possible causes Frost, storm, cold winds, or lack of a pollinator nearby in the case of trees which are not self-pollinating.

Treatment Protect early flowering fruits with netting. Provide shelter from cold winds. Make sure there are suitable pollinator varieties nearby.

Reverting

Possible causes A reverted green shoot growing among variegated foliage. This is a natural phenomenon.

Treatment Cut out the reverted shoot or branch before it takes over, as it invariably will, since it is usually the stronger grower.

CHAPTER 9

Tree Guide

Trees for Special Purposes

In the calendar section, lists of trees dealt with seasonal interests of flowers, foliage, fruits and bark. Lists of trees for special purposes now follow. The trees have been selected from the 'Tree Guides' which make up a large proportion of this chapter.

As previously mentioned, the key to success is to match trees as nearly as possible to soil and site conditions.

TREES FOR CONTAINERS

Broadleaved
Acer palmatum	Japanese Maple
Arbutus unedo	Strawberry Tree
Betula pendula various	Birch
Cotoneaster × 'Hybridus Pendulus'	Weeping Cotoneaster
Ilex × *altaclarensis* various	Holly
Laburnum × *watereri* 'Vossii'	Golden Chain
Malus various	Apple
Prunus 'Pendula Rosea'	Weeping Cherry
Prunus various	Plum and Cherry
Pyrus communis	Pear
Rhus typhina	Stag's Horn Sumach
Salix caprea 'Kilmarnock'	Kilmarnock Willow
Sophora tetraptera 'Grandiflora'	Pagoda Tree
Trachycarpus fortunei	Chusan Palm

Conifers
Abies koreana	Korean Fir
Calocedrus decurrens	Incense Cedar
Chamaecyparis lawsoniana 'Ellwoodii'	Lawson Cypress
Cryptomeria 'Elegans'	Japanese Cedar
Juniperus communis	Juniper
Picea glauca 'Albertiana Conica'	Spruce
Pinus mugo	Mountain Pine
Taxus baccata 'Standishii'	Yew
Thuja occidentalis 'Rheingold'	Arborvitae

TREES FOR SMALL GARDENS

Broadleaved

Acer Palmatum	Japanese Maple
Arbutus unedo	Strawberry Tree
Cornus mas	Cornelian Cherry
Cotoneaster × 'Hybridus Pendulus'	Weeping Cotoneaster
Ilex × *altaclarensis*	Holly
Magnolia × *soulangiana*	Magnolia
Morus nigra	Mulberry
Prunus 'Pendula Rosea'	Weeping Cherry
Salix caprea 'Kilmarnock'	Kilmarnock Willow

Conifers

Abies koreana	Korean Fir
Chamaecyparis lawsoniana 'Ellwoodii'	Lawson Cypress
Cryptomeria japonica 'Elegans Compacta'	Japanese Cedar
Juniperus communis various	Juniper
Picea glauca 'Albertiana Conica'	Spruce
Pinus mugo various	Mountain Pine
Taxus baccata 'Standishii'	Yew
Thuja occidentalis 'Rheingold'	Arborvitae

QUICK-GROWING TREES

Broadleaved

Amalanchier lamarckii	Snowy Mespilus
Corylus maxima 'Purpurea'	Purple-leaved Filbert
Cotoneaster × 'Hybridus Pendulus'	Weeping Cotoneaster
Cytisus battandieri	Moroccan Broom
Laburnum × *watereri* 'Vossii'	Golden Chain
Malus various	Crab Apple
Prunus cerasifera 'Pissardii'	Purple-leaved Plum
Pyrus communis various	Pear
Rhus typhina	Stag's Horn Sumach
Robinia pseudoacacia 'Frisia'	Golden False Acacia
Sorbus aria 'Lutescens'	Whitebeam
Sorbus aucuparia	Mountain Ash

Conifers

Cupressocyparis leylandii 'Castlewellan'	Golden Leyland Cypress

TREES FOR COLD SITES

(A) = cold winter tolerant – can withstand low temperatures in the dormant season.

(B) = can tolerate cold year round as well as strong winds. Good at the coast.

(C) = can survive east-facing sites without serious scorching. Sites where there is early morning sun after overnight frost can all too easily bring about a too rapid thaw – this causes serious damage and blackening to buds and foliage.

Broadleaved

Betula pendula 'Youngii'	Young's Weeping Birch (A) (C)
Crataegus various	Thorn (A) (B) (C)
Fagus sylvatica various	Beech (A) (C)
Ilex × altaclarensis various	Holly (A) (B)
Laburnum × watereri 'Vossii'	Golden Chain (A) (B) (C)
Malus various	Crab Apple (A) (B)
Prunus cerasifera 'Pissardii'	Purple-leaved Plum (A) (B) (C)
Salix caprea 'Kilmarnock'	Kilmarnock Willow (A) (B) (C)
Sorbus aria 'Lutescens'	Whitebeam (A) (B) (C)
Sorbus aucuparia	Mountain Ash (A) (B) (C)

Conifers

Chamaecyparis lawsoniana 'Ellwoodii'	Lawson Cypress (A) (B)
Cupressocyparis leylandii 'Castlewellan'	Golden Leyland Cypress (A) (B)
Juniperus communis 'Suecica'	Juniper (A) (B) (C)
Pinus mugo	Mountain Pine (A) (B) (C)
Taxus baccata various	Yew (A) (B)

TREES TO AVOID IN TOWN GARDENS

Broadleaved

Cercidiphyllum japonicum	Katsura Tree
Eucalyptus niphophila	Snow Gum
Koelreuteria paniculata	Golden Rain Tree
Tamarix gallica	Common Tamarisk

Conifers

Abies koreana	Korean Fir
Picea glauca 'Albertiana Conica'	Spruce

TREES FOR WALLS

Broadleaved
Arbutus unedo	Strawberry Tree
Cercidiphyllum japonicum	Katsura Tree
Cercis siliquastrum	Judas Tree
Cytisus battandieri	Moroccan Broom
Ilex × altaclarensis	Holly
Laburnum × watereri 'Vossii'	Golden Chain
Malus various	Apple
Malus various	Crab Apple
Morus nigra	Mulberry
Parrotia persica	Persian Ironwood
Prunus various	Plum and Cherry
Pyrus communis various	Pear
Sophora tetraptera 'Grandiflora'	Pagoda Tree

DROUGHT-TOLERANT TREES

Broadleaved
Cercis siliquastrum	Judas Tree
Crataegus prunifolia	Plum-leaf Thorn
Cytisus battandieri	Moroccan Broom
Eucalyptus niphophila	Snow Gum
Gleditsia triacanthos 'Sunburst'	Golden Honey Locust
Koelreuteria paniculata 'Fastigiata'	Golden Rain Tree
Laburnum × watereri 'Vossii'	Golden Chain
Rhus typhina	Stag's Horn Sumach
Robinia pseudoacacia 'Frisia'	Golden False Acacia
Sorbus aucuparia	Mountain Ash

Conifers
Juniperus communis 'Suecica'	Juniper
Taxus baccata 'Standishii'	Yew

TREES FOR SCREENS AND WINDBREAKS

Broadleaved

Amelanchier lamarckii	Snowy Mespilus
Corylus maxima 'Purpurea'	Purple-leaved Filbert
Crataegus various	Thorn
Ilex × *altaclarensis* various	Holly
Laburnum various	Golden Chain
Malus various	Crab Apple
Prunus cerasifera 'Pissardii'	Purple-leaved Plum
Sorbus aria various	Whitebeam
Sorbus aucuparia	Mountain Ash
Tamarix gallica	Common Tamarisk

Conifers

Cupressocyparis leylandii 'Castlewellan'	Golden Leyland Cypress

TREES TOLERANT OF WET, HEAVY SOILS

Broadleaved

Betula pendula 'Youngii'	Young's Weeping Birch
Cornus mas	Cornelian Cherry
Corylus maxima 'Purpurea'	Purple-leaved Filbert
Cotoneaster × 'Hybridus Pendulus'	Weeping Cotoneaster
Crataegus prunifolia	Plum-leaf Thorn
Ilex × *altaclarensis* 'Camellifolia'	Holly
Laburnum × *watereri* 'Vossii'	Laburnum Golden Chain
Magnolia × *soulangiana*	Magnolia
Prunus cerasifera 'Pissardii'	Purple-leaved Plum
Salix caprea 'Kilmarnock'	Kilmarnock Willow
Sorbus aria 'Lutescens'	Whitebeam
Sorbus aucuparia	Mountain Ash
Syringa vulgaris various	Lilac

Conifers

Chamaecyparis lawsoniana 'Ellwoodii'	Lawson Cypress
Taxus baccata 'Standishii'	Yew

TREES FOR CHALK SOILS

Broadleaved

Betula pendula 'Youngii'	Young's Weeping Bush
Cercis siliquastrum	Judas Tree
Cornus mas	Cornelian Cherry
Corylus maxima 'Purpurea'	Purple-leaved Filbert
Cotoneaster × 'Hybridus Pendulus'	Weeping Cotoneaster
Crataegus prunifolia	Plum-leaved Thorn
Cytisus battandieri	Moroccan Broom
Fagus sylvatica 'Purpurea Pendula'	Weeping Purple Beech
Ilex × *altaclarensis* 'Camellifolia'	Holly
Laburnum × *watereri* 'Vossii'	Golden Chain
Malus sylvestris	Apple
Malus various	Crab Apple
Prunus cerasifera 'Pissardii'	Purple-leaved Plum
Prunus 'Pendula Rosea'	Weeping Cherry
Prunus various	Plums and Cherries
Pyrus communis	Pear
Pyrus salicifolia 'Pendula'	Weeping Silver Pear
Rhus typhina	Stag's Horn Sumach
Robinia pseudoacacia 'Frisia'	Golden False Acacia
Salix caprea 'Kilmarnock'	Kilmarnock Willow
Sorbus aria 'Lutescens'	Whitebeam
Sorbus aucuparia	Mountain Ash
Syringa vulgaris	Lilac

Conifers

Chamaecyparis lawsoniana 'Ellwoodii'	Lawson Cypress
Cupressocyparis leylandii 'Castlewellan'	Golden Leyland Cypress
Pinus mugo	Mountain Pine
Taxus baccata 'Standishii'	Yew
Thuja occidentalis 'Rheingold'	Arborvitae

BROADLEAVED TREES

Acer Palmatum

Japanese Maple
Hardiness HR2
Deciduous tree or shrub

Description Attractive small rounded tree; ht to 15ft (4.5m). Normally grown as a bush or standard. Noted for its autumn tints. The leaves — five or seven lobed — are bright green in summer and turn to orange and red in autumn, at which time mature trees carry a bonus of reddish-pink keys.

Varieties Noteworthy small trees and large shrubs descended from *Acer palmatum* are *A.p.* 'heptalobum Osakazuki' — its green leaves turn to brilliant flame and scarlet, and *A.p.* 'Senkaki',

Fig 66 Acer palmatum – *known for its autumn tints.*

the coral bark maple – coral red stems and yellow autumn foliage. Both reach ht 10–12ft (3–3.5m) or more.

Other particularly good Japanese maples include varieties of *Acer japonicum*. They are closely related to *A.palmatum* and of similar size: *A.j.* 'Aconitifolium' – crimson autumn foliage; *A.j.* 'Vitifolium' – red autumn leaves.

Position and use Plant Japanese maples in full sun or partial shade, sheltered from cold or drying winds. Avoid east-facing positions open to early morning sun where young leaves injured by too rapid thawing after overnight frost will remain blemished throughout the season.

Acid to near neutral, free-draining but moist, soil is preferred.

Suitable for planting in tubs on a patio. Looks well as a specimen in the lawn and mixed with shrubs in the border as a focal point.

Treatment Plant out Japanese maples during autumn or spring using container-raised stock. Containers are best planted up in spring. Protect young foliage from late spring frosts and wind for the first few years at least. Little pruning is needed beyond cutting out any dead or dying shoots/branches – work which is best carried out in autumn, and definitely not to be attempted in late winter or early spring, otherwise there is a risk of bleeding.

Propagation Sow *A.palmatum* species in autumn or early winter, to allow time for chilling. Graft named varieties like *A.p.* 'Senkaki' on to seedling rootstocks of *A.palmatum* during March or April.

Treat *A.japonicum* seed as above. Likewise graft named varieties such as *A.j.* 'Aconitifolium' on to seedling rootstocks of *A.japonicum* in spring.

Problems Red spider mite can be troublesome in dry weather. Vulnerable to scorching of leaves due to wind or frost.

Amelanchier Lamarckii

Snowy Mespilus, June Berry
(sometimes listed as
A.canadensis)
Hardiness HR2
Deciduous tree or shrub

Description A much under-rated small dome-shaped or spreading tree; ht to 20ft (6m). Grown as a bush or standard, and sometimes as a multi-stemmed tree or shrub. A mass of white blossom is produced in spring over a two to three week period. Black, small rounded fruits crop in mid-summer. The leaves are quite a feature – coppery coloured when young, turning to scarlet in autumn prior to leaf fall.

Varieties *A.l.* 'Rubescens' – rather uncommon with pink-tinged flowers. Otherwise similar in habit, size and leaf colouring to *A.lamarckii*. It is not readily available, but well worth seeking out.

A.laevis is useful – similar in size, habit and flower colour to *A.lamarckii*, but with pink young leaves and more subdued autumn tints.

Position and use Snowy mespilus grows well in sun or light partial shade. For best results and a

Fig 67 Amelanchier makes a good alternative to flowering cherry which it resembles – with the added bonus of fruit and foliage colour.

long flowering period, avoid very exposed – as well as east-facing – cold sites when planting.

Any reasonably fertile, well drained soil that remains moist and cool in summer will normally suffice. But the richest autumn colourings are usually found on lime-free to neutral soil.

This tree makes a fine focal point, planted singly in grass, but also looks good set among shrubs or ground cover.

Treatment Plant during autumn or spring, but always use container-raised trees for setting out in spring. Plant up containers in March/April. No more than average shelter and protection is required for newly planted trees. No special pruning is needed, beyond cutting out dead wood and pruning to shape in autumn if necessary. Remove suckers if these proliferate around the base of the trunk.

Propagation All can be raised from layers pegged down in early autumn – ready for severing and lifting a year later. Alternatively, carefully lift rooted suckers in autumn and pot up or plant out. Grow on layers/rooted suckers for two or three years, overwintering pot grown plants under cover, or giving them extra root protection.

Increase from seed sown in late summer under a cold frame is possible, but seedlings tend to be more variable than with layers or suckers.

Problems Occasionally attacked by fireblight. Normally free of pests.

Arbutus Unedo

Strawberry Tree
Hardiness HR2
Evergreen tree or shrub

Description A choice, bushy wide-topped small tree, ht to 20ft (6m). Usually grown with a branching crown on a short trunk. Although slow growing, is very useful for providing autumn and winter interest.

The strawberry tree is unusual in that it produces clusters of pendent ivory-white flowers, along with orange-red ornamental strawberry-like ripening fruits, developed from the previous season's flowers. Flowers and ripening fruit appear between October and December in the main. Shiny evergreen leaves provide an excellent foil for flowers and fruit to relieve winter drabness. The trunks of mature trees are curiously and distinctively gnarled.

Varieties *A.u.* 'Rubra' has pink-flushed flowers and a more compact habit than *A.unedo*, but is similar in other respects.

Position and use Strawberry trees are equally at home in full sun or light partial shade. Give them a sheltered site, protected from freezing cold or drying winds. They will grow and flourish in cool districts provided they are given a sunny south or west-facing wall and winter frosts are not too severe. Avoid east-facing aspects.

Free-draining, humus-rich, peaty or leafy moist acid soil is preferred. However, unlike many other members of the heather family to which they belong, strawberry trees can adapt to chalk soils, provided they are neither too dry nor too shallow.

Looks well in a sheltered border as an accent plant, and in a container for patio display.

Treatment Plant out during October and November or from March to May. Use container-raised trees. Plant up containers in spring. Protect newly planted trees from wind. If possible use rainwater in preference to mains supply for watering. Prune trees to shape and remove any dead or dying branches in late spring and summer, keeping cutting down to a minimum.

Propagation *A.unedo* can be raised from seed sown in spring under cover – using ericaceous seed compost. Prick out singly into small pots of ericaceous potting compost. Grow on for two or three years giving frame protection in winter.

Fig 68   The evergreen Arbutus unedo *needs a mild climate and shelter where it can best display its delightful combination of strawberry-like red fruits and pink or white flowers in late autumn.*

All can be raised from cuttings – and cuttings are certainly best for *A.u.* 'Rubra'. Take semi-ripewood node or heel cuttings in July. Make them about 4in (10cm) long and use a rooting preparation – they can be tricky. Insert in a 50:50 sand:peat cutting mixture and root in warmth at 60–65°F (16–18°C). Pot up when rooted and treat as for seedlings.

Problems Provided sheltered from freezing winds, generally trouble free.

Betula Pendula 'Youngii'

Young's Weeping Birch
Hardiness HRI
Deciduous tree

Description A small dome-shaped tree of considerable charm and character; ht to 15ft (4.5m). Usually grown as a weeping standard.

Important features of interest: eye-catching whitish bark year-round – seen to best advantage in winter; pleasing outline; pleasant green summer foliage, turning to yellow in autumn; and greenish-yellow spring catkins.

Varieties A short selection from the many kinds of birch: *B.pendula*, the common silver birch – ht over 30ft (9m). Of broadly columnar outline with slender pendulous branchlets and outstanding silvery bark. Foliage and catkins similar to Young's weeping birch. *B.p.* 'Fastigiata' very like *B.pendula* in many respects, but much narrower in shape. *B.p.* 'Purpurea' is a slow-growing, rather striking purple-leaved form.

A closely related birch *B.jacquemontii* has particularly brilliant white bark – otherwise similar to the common silver birch.

Position and use Green-leaved varieties will grow well in sun or light shade, but give the purple-leaved birch a sunny spot for best results. Undemanding about shelter, but avoid very exposed positions if growth rate and shape are not to suffer. Birch can adapt to most sites.

87

Being a tree native to the British Isles, birch can tolerate shallow as well as heavy and chalky soils, but prefers a medium, moist loam which is reasonably fertile and well drained.

Use As a specimen tree in a lawn; in the front garden; in the shrub border; in the hedgerow; in the roadside verge; as a patio tree in a tub or bonsai dish. Birch mix well with heathers and rhododendrons and look attractive under-planted with spring bulbs like crocus and daffodils.

Treatment Plant in autumn or spring. Use container-raised stock for any late planting after March. Plant up containers in early spring. Don't prune birch in late winter or spring due to the risk of bleeding. Little pruning is normally needed – keep cutting to a minimum.

Propagation Sow seed of *B.pendula* in spring – it needs chilling. Or use self-sown seedlings. Pot up singly and grow on for two or three years.

Graft named varieties like Young's weeping and purple birch on to common birch seedling rootstocks during March or April.

Problems Aphid and caterpillars can be troublesome, but spraying is not normally necessary except in severe attacks. Rust occasionally attacks – it looks unsightly and can cause permanent damage. See page 77–8.

Cercidiphyllum Japonicum

Katsura Tree
Hardiness HR3
Deciduous tree

Description A medium to large tree; ht to 30ft (9m) or more, with a spreading rounded or broadly oval habit. Usually grown as a standard, but makes an attractive multi-stemmed tree of more manageable size for modern gardens. The main feature is the foliage – heart-shaped leaves open out bright pink in spring, gradually turning

sea green in summer – through to shades of pink, red and yellow in autumn.

Variety The closely related but less common *C.magnificum* is of similar size and habit. The leaves are considerably larger, but lack the bright pink shades on opening. In autumn they turn yellow without the characteristic red and pink colourings of *C.japonicum*. Also the bark is appreciably smoother.

Position and use The best colourings are likely in sunny situations, but light shade is no serious drawback. The ideal position is a south or west-facing aspect sheltered by trees or buildings from cold north and east winds. Provide a sheltered spot. Although the trees are hardy, the young leaves are easily scorched by cold winds and late spring frosts.

An acid soil, or one with a low lime content, bringing the pH up to neutral, will ensure the best leaf colouring, but deep chalk soils are tolerated. A medium, free-draining loam, well enriched with peat or leaf mould is the ideal. But these trees will adapt to light sandy or gravelly soils.

Fig 69 The little known Cercidiphyllum japonicum *colours best on acid soil and puts on a fine display of autumn leaf tints.*

The main use is as a single specimen tree in grass.

Treatment Using container-raised trees, plant in autumn or spring. Of necessity protect from cold wind and frost immediately after setting out until established. Minimal autumn pruning to shape is required. To keep a Katsura tree small, cut out the main stem when young and grow on as a multi stem large shrub.

Propagation Sow seeds in late winter, chill, then bring into warmth of 60–65°F (16–18°C) to germinate. Prick out singly into small pots. Grow on for two or three years before planting out, overwintering under cover and potting on as necessary.

Problems Provided sheltered, trouble free.

Cercis Siliquastrum

Judas Tree
Hardiness HR2
Deciduous tree or shrub

Description A very desirable small to medium-sized rounded tree; ht to 20ft (6m). Grown as a bush and as a short standard. Alternatively it makes a very pleasing multi-stemmed, basal branching shrub; ht about 10ft (3m). The pink pea-shaped flowers are very freely produced along bare stems and branches in April and May, as the rounded green leaves unfold. Incidentally, the flowers were used years ago as an ingredient in salads. During summer, thin red pods are produced and hold fast to give colour and interest during autumn and winter.

Varieties Look for *C.s.* 'Alba', a white-flowered variety, and the unusual deep purple *C.s.* 'Bodnant'.

Position and use Where possible plant in a sunny, warm and well-sheltered spot – where the branches can get properly ripened. This en-

Fig 70 Cercis siliquastrum, makes an attractive small tree, producing masses of pink pea-shaped flowers on bare branches in spring, followed by warm leaf tints in autumn.

courages free flowering and a good set of pods with subsequent full colouring. A south aspect is the ideal, with west-facing a good second best.

A well-drained, light to medium fertile loam, preferably not too rich, will suit. Chalky soil if not too shallow is no handicap, but avoid wet, heavy ground.

The Judas tree makes an attractive specimen in grass and hard-surfaced areas; looks well as a wall tree and when planted among shrubs; makes a useful tub tree or shrub.

Treatment Like other members of the pea family, the Judas tree resents root disturbance. So buy container-raised plants. Ideally set out in autumn while there is still some warmth in the soil. Plant up containers in spring using soil-based potting compost. Little pruning is necessary beyond shortening straggly stems and thinning out overcrowded shoots in autumn.

Propagation   Pre-soak the seeds in tepid water for six hours, then sow singly in small pots – in spring. Germinate at 65° (18°C). Harden off and move out under a frame. Grow on for two years, potting on each spring.

Problems   Unlikely.

Cornus Mas

Cornelian Cherry
Hardiness HR2
Deciduous tree or shrub

Description   A delightful, but largely ignored, small to medium-sized tree; ht to 18ft (5m), with a spreading habit. It is frequently grown as a bushy basal-branching tree or short standard. When trained as a shrub a ht of about 10ft (3m) is average. Masses of small yellow flowers appear during February and early March on bare leafless branches, at a time when there is not a lot of colour about. Sometimes the flowers are followed by rounded, reddish fruits. The medium to large green leaves take on bronzy-red autumn tints.

Varieties   Although usually grown as shrubs the following varieties will make useful small trees. They all have attractive summer foliage – the winter flowers are less pronounced. *C.m.* 'Aurea' – soft golden yellow leaves; *C.m.* 'Elegantissima' – variegated green and yellow-tinged pink leaves; *C.m.* 'Variegata' – white-margined green leaves.

Position and use   Although best in sun, will grow well when shaded for part of the day. Avoid heavy shade and dense overhanging branches. Plant in a sheltered spot protected from freezing northerly or easterly winds or there is a risk of winter flowers being spoilt. By a similar token, avoid east-facing sites where any frozen flowers are likely to be damaged by a too quick thaw.

Any reasonably fertile, average garden soil will suit. The Cornelian cherry will even thrive in chalky soil, provided there is adequate soil depth.

These are useful small trees for planting among shrubs and ground cover. Also for fronting other trees.

Treatment   Plant out ideally in October and November. Spring planting is best ignored, otherwise trees are put under stress at flowering time. Protect newly planted trees from cold winds in their first winter/early spring, especially if in flower. No special pruning is needed beyond cutting out dead wood and keeping trees in good shape. Work best carried out after flowering.

Propagation   Increase *C.mas* from either seeds or cuttings. Sow ripe seeds in autumn or winter and chill. Germinate in warmth at about 60°F (16°C) – it may take up to eighteen months. Prick out singly into small pots and grow on for two to three years.

All the above varieties of Cornelian cherry can be raised from 4in (10cm) long semi-ripewood heel or node cuttings, taken in July or early August. Root in warmth at 60°F (16°C). Pot up singly when rooted and grow on as for seedlings.

Problems   Unlikely.

Corylus Maxima 'Purpurea'

Purple-leaf Filbert
Purple-leaf Hazel Nut
Hardiness HRI
Deciduous tree or shrub

Description   A spreading, rounded or domed small tree; ht to about 15ft (4.5m). Usually grown as a bush or half-standard. Noted for its fine purple foliage and large leaves which provide spring and summer colour. Long purple catkins which sway and quiver in the breeze among bare branches provide an added bonus in late winter and spring. In favoured sites and mild climates, nuts are produced in autumn.

Varieties   Close relatives of the above include a couple of varieties descended from the native

Fig 71 The purple foliage of Corylus maxima 'Purpurea' provides a striking contrast to nearby yellow foliage.

British hazel. The first of these, the yellow nut, C. avellana 'Aurea' – ht to 10ft (3m) or more – has attractive soft golden yellow summer foliage. In spring, yellow fluffy catkins are carried on bare branches. The second – the corkscrew hazel, C.a. 'Contorta' – ht to 10ft (3m) and more. This tree is something of a curiosity and is perhaps best seen in late winter when its twisted, corkscrew-like bare branches are exposed to full view. The effect is further heightened by pendulous, yellow catkins which highlight in the sun.

Position and use Plant up in sunny positions, protected from cold winds, especially from the north and east. The yellow nut grows best in partial or light shade.

Any reasonably fertile soil will suffice – ranging from light loams to heavy soils – provided that these are well drained. Chalk soils are no problem.

The purple-leaf filbert makes a useful specimen plant in grass and looks well in a shrub border – contrasted against a pale backdrop or with such as the yellow nut. The corkscrew hazel is effective as a waterside feature.

Treatment Plant between autumn and spring. Cut back the new season's growth by about half after planting to encourage branching. Subsequently, shorten the new season's growth by one-third to a half each autumn. In later years, aim to remove some of the older wood annually.

Propagation Although hazels can be increased from seed, the varieties listed here do not come true to form and are best layered. Peg down layers in autumn. Sever and lift when rooted – in about twelve months. Pot up and grow on for two or three years, protecting the roots from winter frost.

Problems Leaf-eating caterpillars and weevils can be destructive, although spraying is not normally necessary.

Cotoneaster x 'Hybridus Pendulus'

Weeping Cotoneaster
Hardiness HRI
Evergreen tree or shrub

Description A very popular dome-shaped small tree, ht 5–8ft (1.5–2.5m). Normally grown as a weeping standard. The chief attractions are: masses of bright red berries which give colour during autumn and winter; glossy evergreen willow-like leaves which set off the berries; and white hawthorn-like slightly scented flowers in June.

Varieties Although the cotoneaster family is large and varied, there are few varieties of tree size – the best of which are now discussed. C. 'Cornubia' – ht 15–20ft (4.5–6m) – a rounded or spreading semi-evergreen tree. The white June flowers are followed by clusters of big red autumn berries which persist through into winter. *C.frigidus* – ht to 15ft (4.5m) – makes a quick-growing semi-evergreen tree. White June flowers are followed by heavy clusters of crimson berries. *C.* 'Rothschildianus' – ht to 12ft (3.5m) – forms a pleasing small evergreen tree with pale green pointed willow-like leaves. White June flowers are followed by creamy yellow berries which last well into winter.

Position and use Sunny sites are best, but these particular cotoneasters will flower and berry well in partial or light shade. Preferably plant in a sheltered position protected from north and east winds – this is most important with the evergreen varieties. These should not be given an east-facing aspect, exposed to early morning sun.

Any average garden soil, including chalk, will suit.

The above varieties are all suitable for use: as single specimen trees in grass or hard-surfaced areas; to plant among shrubs; and to set out in tubs for patio decoration.

Treatment Preferably plant out in autumn, but spring is satisfactory, provided container-raised trees are used. Prune both evergreen and semi-

Fig 72 Crataegus. The flowers appear in May and June.

evergreen varieties in spring. No special routine is necessary beyond cutting out dead or weak overcrowded shoots and keeping trees in shape.

Propagation Since seed-raised cotoneasters tend to be very variable, cuttings, layers and grafts are preferred. Graft *C.* 'Hybridus Pendulus' by top working on *C.frigidus* rootstock in March or April. Increase the other three varieties by rooting 4in (10cm) semi-ripewood heel cuttings in late July/early August in a closed frame. Pot up singly into small pots when rooted, usually by the following spring. Grow on for two or three years.

Problems Look for aphid and scale insects and spray if they show signs of getting out of hand. Fireblight can attack large fruited varieties. See page 77.

Crataegus Prunifolia

Plum-leaf Thorn
Hardiness HRI
Deciduous tree

Description A pleasing small to medium-sized tree with a compact, rounded crown; ht to 20ft (6m). Normally grown as a standard. The plum-leaf thorn deserves to be better known and more widely grown. An important feature is the oval green leaves, with glossy upper surface and matt reverse, turning to glorious orange, flame and scarlet shades in autumn. Clusters of white, scented, typical hawthorn flowers appear in May and June, to be followed in autumn by scarlet haws/berries. These last well into winter.

Varieties Some of the best thorns include: *C.coccinea*, the scarlet haw (syn *C.pedicellata*) – ht to 20ft (6m). Similar to plum-leaf thorn, but of a more spreading habit with redder autumn tints and much brighter scarlet haws. *C.monogyna* 'Pendula Rosea', ht 20ft (6m). The crown is loosely rounded. Noted for its pendulous habit and pink flowers during May and June. *C.oxyacantha* 'Paul's Scarlet' or 'Coccinea Plena' – ht 20ft

(6m) – carries double scarlet flowers in May and June. *C.o.* 'Rosea Flore Pleno' – a double pink flowered form of 'Paul's Scarlet'.

Position and use   For preference, site thorns in sun, but they will adapt well to shade. Being very hardy they can tolerate fairly exposed positions.

Any reasonable garden soil, including chalk, will suit.

Thorns have many uses – from making fine single specimens in grass and hard-surfaced areas to planting among shrubs; from making effective screens to displaying in containers – and training.

Treatment   Plant thorns in autumn or spring, making sure that standards are securely staked and tied – vital when grown in exposed situations. Little regular pruning is required beyond autumn trimming to shape, and thinning out weak, inward growing and crossing branches.

Propagation   Choice named varieties are normally budded in July/August; or grafted in March – on to seedling rootstocks. Use *C.monogyna* rootstock for *C.m.* 'Pendula Rosea' and *C. oxyacantha* for the rest. Collect fresh seed in autumn and store in damp sand for eighteen months outdoors – in a vermin- and bird-proof place. Sow the seeds in spring under cover. Prick out seedlings singly into pots and grow on for two years before budding, or two-and-a-half years before grafting.

Problems   Keep leaf-eating caterpillars in check with insecticide sprays. Occasionally fireblight will attack, and mildew is fairly common. See page 77.

Cytisus Battandieri

Moroccan Broom
Hardiness HR3
Deciduous tree or shrub

Description   A highly desirable small tree of upright habit, ht to about 13ft (4m). Commonly grown as a wall-trained tree – and makes an attractive standard too, unlike most other brooms which are shrub-like in character. This broom also differs in that the broad three-lobed leaves are covered attractively in silky, silvery, grey hair – giving a whitish sheen to their appearance. Golden-yellow, pineapple-scented pea-like flowers are carried in striking cone-shaped clusters – usually at their best during late May and June.

Varieties   *C.* 'Porlock'; ht to 10ft (3m). A semi-evergreen variety with light green leaves and scented yellow flowers during May and June. Sometimes grown as a wall-trained tree.

Position and use   Both these brooms are seen at their best in warm, sunny situations. Give them a sheltered site, backed by walls or trees or shrubs. The ideal is to reserve a south or west-facing aspect, protected from cold north or east winds. In cool areas they must have wall protection.

A free-draining light sandy to medium not-too-rich loam will suit. Chalky soils are no impediment – provided they are not too shallow. Avoid heavy, wet or very rich soils. They either encourage root rotting or excessive growth at the expense of flowers.

The Moroccan broom is outstanding and makes an excellent single specimen in grass. Also very effective against a wall, as is *C.* 'Porlock'. Set them near to windows where the scent can waft indoors.

Treatment   Brooms strongly resent root disturbance – so always buy container-raised stock. Plant out while small to minimize any setback. Set out in final positions in autumn. As soon as flowering is over, remove misplaced and weak growths. In the case of wall-trained specimens, tie in strong new shoots.

Propagation   Increase Moroccan broom from seed. In spring, pre-soak the seed in warm, but not hot, water for four to six hours before sowing singly in small pots of seed compost. Germinate at 60–65°F (16–18°C). Harden off the seedlings and move out under a frame. Grow on for six to eight weeks before removing the frame lights to acclimatize the young plants to outdoor conditions in readiness for planting out in September/October.

Raise C. 'Porlock' by taking 3–4in (7.5–10cm) heel cuttings in August. Root in warmth using a cutting compost of equal parts peat and sand. Pot up singly into 4in (10cm) containers. Over-winter under cover. Harden off in spring. Grow on until autumn. Then plant out.

Problems   Reasonably trouble free.

Davidia Involucrata

Pocket Handkerchief Tree
Dove Tree
Hardiness HR3
Deciduous tree

Description   A very distinct and rather unusual small to medium-sized tree – cone-shaped when young, becoming rounded or domed with age. Ht to 25ft (7.5m). Usually grown as a standard, but can sometimes be found, as a basal branching bush tree. The true flowers are overpowered by pairs of white or ivory handkerchief-like bracts – eye-catching during May. The reason for the popular name is not hard to find. The bracts are showy for about three weeks. They are unlikely to be produced on trees less than ten to twelve years old. The almost lime-like green leaves are not unattractive either.

Variety   The only readily obtainable variety is D.i. 'Vilmoriniana'. It is almost identical to the original handkerchief tree, the main difference being in its leaves – these are smooth on the underside as opposed to felted.

Position and use   Best in sun, but will tolerate partial shade and still put on a good show. Try to select a sheltered site where strong winds and late spring frosts are unlikely.

A deep, fertile, free-draining moist soil that does not dry out badly during prolonged drought is needed.

The handkerchief tree makes a spectacular specimen grown in a well-kept lawn – especially when seen against a contrasting backdrop. Also looks well planted amongst shrubs and ground cover.

Treatment   Plant in autumn. Handkerchief trees resent root disturbance – so be sure to buy container-raised young trees. Avoid large trees, which are slow to re-establish in new positions. Special pruning is not normally necessary beyond cutting out dead or weak shoots in autumn.

Propagation   Provided suitable branches are within reach of the ground, layering in autumn is the best method of increase. Peg down young stems, preferably into a container of potting compost, and keep moist during the summer months. Sever and lift with care when rooted – in about two years.

Otherwise propagate by taking 4in (10cm) heel cuttings during July/early August. Root under a shaded frame in soil consisting of equal parts peat and sand. Pot up singly when rooted and grow on for two or three years, overwintering under cover.

D.involucrata can be raised from seed – a high proportion of which are likely to be identical with the parent. Sow in containers in spring or summer. Keep moist and shaded in a frame for eighteen to thirty months – until germinated. Prick out singly into pots and grow on for two or three years.

Problems   Unlikely.

Eucalyptus Niphophila

Snow Gum
Hardiness HR2
Evergreen tree

Description A small to medium-sized rounded or oval tree; ht to about 25ft (7.5m). Usually grown as a standard, but can be kept compact by pollarding. Slow growing up to five years, then speeding up. The foliage is the main attraction. The leaves on young trees are reddish-brown. They turn to a glaucous blue-green on adult trees. The bark is also important. It is blue-white on young shoots. When four to five years old, the bark peels and sheds each autumn, to reveal cream, ivory or grey underbark. The result is a pleasant mottling. Groups of white flowers appear during June.

Varieties *E.gunnii*, the cider gum, makes a big oval or spreading tree; ht 50ft (15m) or more — and is the eucalyptus perhaps most often seen. It is fairly hardy. The juvenile leaves are silvery, blue-green and rounded. The adult leaves are pointed and glaucous mid-green. *E.pauciflora*, the cabbage gum, is a quick-growing and somewhat larger alternative to the snow gum; ht 30ft (9m). Colourings are more muted.

Position and use Reserve sunny and warm situations for eucalyptus. They need shelter and protection, especially in winter. If possible plant them in south or west facing spot out of reach of cold north or east winds.

A light to medium, not-too-rich, free-draining soil suits well. Avoid wet soils and shallow chalk soils.

Where space allows, eucalyptus make good specimen trees in grass. They can look well in a shrub border when dwarfed by annual pollarding.

Treatment Plant out as small 12–18in (30–45cm) high pot-raised seedlings during summer. Stake and tie firmly for several years until established. Protect during winter by covering the roots and lower stems with straw until well established. Similarly, protect young trees from wind during winter — by using fine mesh netting on a light frame. Where the aim is to restrict tree size, prune new shoots back by half each summer. If pruning has been neglected, or trees have been allowed to grow too big, they can be cut down to near ground level in spring before growth recommences.

Propagation During autumn, sow seeds in small pots — singly. Chill for eight weeks in a cold frame, or in a vermin-proof box outdoors. Then bring into warmth to germinate at 60°F (16°C). Harden off in late spring and grow for a further four to six weeks before planting out in their final positions.

Problems Damping off amongst seedlings can be a problem. See page 77.

Fig 73   Eucalyptus niphophila is one of the best of the blue gums for garden use, being smaller and hardier than most.

Fig 74   The dome-shaped purple-leaved Fagus sylvatica 'Purpurea Pendula' provides a striking contrast to trees of conical or columnar outline with golden foliage.

Fagus Sylvatica 'Purpurea Pendula'

Weeping Purple Beech
Hardiness HRI
Deciduous tree

Description   A popular dome-shaped small to medium-sized tree; ht to about 20ft (6m). Usually grown as a weeping standard. Undoubtedly the main feature is the striking glossy purple foliage. It makes an impact as the leaves open in spring and continue through until autumn. The weeping framework of bare branches provides winter interest as an added bonus.

Varieties   From the many excellent varieties, the following rank with the best of the smaller kinds. (Some beech are too large for the average modern garden.)

F.s. 'Aurea Pendula' has golden yellow leaves, and is similar in size and habit to the weeping purple beech. *F.s.* 'Rohannii' is of rounded or oval habit and makes a medium to large tree; ht to 40ft (12m) – a slow-growing form with purple finely divided leaves. *F.s.* 'Zlatia' makes a medium to large rounded or spreading tree; ht up to 40ft (12m). New leaves open a soft gold, turning green as the season advances.

Position and use   A sunny, open situation is preferable if good foliage is to be ensured.

F.s. 'Aurea Pendula' is the exception – it grows better in light shade. Other varieties are tolerant of partial shade. Avoid very windswept exposed positions.

Beech grow well on most soils of reasonable fertility, including chalk. But avoid wet, clay soil.

The beech mentioned here are all excellent grown as specimens; in grass or hard-surfaced areas or among ground cover.

Treatment   Plant in autumn or spring in well-prepared planting pockets. Make sure that weeping standards especially are firmly staked and tied after planting. No special pruning or other treatment is necessary beyond shortening straggly, weak or misplaced stems during autumn.

Propagation   Graft the varieties mentioned in March/April on to seedling rootstocks of common beech *F.sylvatica*. Seedling rootstocks are raised by sowing ripe seed in containers during autumn and chilling for six to eight weeks. Germinate at 60°F (16°C). Prick out singly into small pots. Harden off. Grow on for two to three years, overwintering the young trees under cover.

Problems   Beech aphid can weaken trees. White cottonwool-like waxy tufts form on leaf undersides accompanied by sticky honeydew. Spray with insecticide in severe outbreaks. Occasional sporadic attacks by coral spot fungus are experienced – but usually no treatment is needed.

Gleditsia Triacanthos 'Sunburst'

Golden Honey Locust
Hardiness HR2
Deciduous tree

Description   A medium-sized spreading, broad-headed tree; ht to 20ft (6m) and over. Usually grown as a standard. Its main attribute is dainty, pinnate leaves which are bright yellow on opening. As they age they gradually turn a greenish-yellow. Unlike other varieties 'Sunburst' is thornless, making it safer to have around the home.

Varieties Many honey locusts grow too big for the average garden. One variety worth searching for is *G.t.* 'Ruby Lace'. Its height and habit is similar to 'Sunburst', but the leaves are a rich purple changing to bronze-green.

Position and use To bring out the best leaf colourings, plant in a warm, sunny spot. But in any event reserve a reasonably sheltered position. Avoid exposed situations and protect from strong or cold winds which are liable to scorch the leaves.

A light to medium fertile loam is preferred, but honey locust will grow satisfactorily in any average soil including chalky.

Honey locusts make useful town trees. They stand up fairly well to drought and normal pollution levels. Both the trees mentioned make excellent specimens planted in grass – but also look well planted in a shrub border.

'Sunburst' is effective if contrasted with, say, purple plum; and 'Ruby Lace', say, in front of a screen of golden Leyland cypress.

Treatment Buy container-raised trees and plant out in autumn or spring. Stake standards firmly. No special treatment or pruning is necessary, beyond removing any deadwood or weak growths in autumn or spring.

Propagation These two varieties are best raised by grafting during March or April on to seedling rootstocks of the common honey locust, *G.triacanthos*. The rootstocks are raised from seed sown in containers during spring and germinated at 60°F (16°C). Pricked out singly into small pots, they are hardened off and grown on for two or three years, overwintering under cover and potting on in spring as it is deemed necessary.

Problems Unlikely.

Ilex x *Altaclarensis* 'Camellifolia'

Holly
Hardiness HRI
Evergreen tree or shrub

Description A very useful small to medium-sized tree; ht to about 20ft (6m). Normally grown as a bush tree or short standard, this holly is narrowly columnar in habit and slow growing. The glossy, dark green leaves are almost spineless. It is worth growing for the foliage alone. Being female, regular crops of large red berries add colour during autumn and winter.

NOTE: Both male and female trees must be planted to ensure berrying.

Varieties Countless varieties are in circulation, such is the popularity of holly. Some of the best: *I.* x *altaclarensis* 'Golden King'; ht to 20ft (6m). A free-berrying female variety – glossy leaves are margined yellow with few spines. *I.aquifolium* 'Argenteo Marginata'; ht to 17ft (5m). Female and berrying with broad white-margined leaves. *I.a.* 'A-M Pendula', or Perry's silver weeping; ht to 15ft (4.5m) – a weeping form. *I.a.* 'Madame Briot'; ht to 17ft (5m). Berrying with spiny, yellow-margined leaves. *I.a* 'Pyramidalis Fructuluteo'; ht 20ft (6m). Carries bright yellow berries; the green leaves are almost spineless.

Position and use Hollies grow well in sun, in semi- and in partial shade. For maximum colour variegated varieties are best in sun. Although hollies are very hardy, they are better with protection from freezing north and east winds and early morning sun. Where possible ignore east-facing sites.

Any reasonable fertile, well-drained soil – including chalky – will support hollies.

Versatility is the keyword when it comes to using hollies. They make fine specimen trees in grass and hard-surfaced areas; look good in groups in the shrub border; are excellent as screens and as hedging; and do well in containers.

Treatment Plant during mild weather in autumn or spring – no matter whether setting out in open ground or in containers. Use container-raised stock. Protect newly set out trees against cold winds and freezing weather using fine mesh netting. Little pruning is needed apart from clipping to shape during summer.

Propagation Most hollies can be raised satisfactorily from 3–4in (8–10cm) semi-ripewood cuttings taken in July and rooted under cover. Alternatively, graft named varieties on to seedling *I.aquifolium*, common holly, during spring or summer. Rootstocks are raised from seed sown in autumn and chilled.

Problems Holly leaf miner can be most disfiguring. Control with insecticide sprays.

Koelreuteria Paniculata

Golden Rain Tree
Pride of India
hardiness HR3
Deciduous tree

Description A small to medium-sized spreading or rounded tree, ht to 25ft (7.5m). Normally grown as a standard. The leaves unfold a very pale yellow, turning to green as the season advances. Yellow autumn tints are evident before leaf fall in most years. During July or August, expect clusters of small yellow flowers. These are followed by green bladder-like fruits, many of which later turn red.

Variety *K.p.* 'Fastigiata' is a narrowly columnar tree, but otherwise very similar to the above.

Position and use Plant in a sunny, sheltered situation – open to the south and west. Avoid cold east or north-facing sites liable to wind.

A free-draining light to medium loam of average fertility will suit. Acid as well as chalk conditions are tolerated, provided they are not too extreme.

Both trees make pleasing specimens when set out in an expanse of grass. Do well in containers.

Treatment Buy young, container-raised trees – nothing too big, 6ft (1.8m) or less – and plant out during autumn or spring. Plant up containers in April or early May. Keep the young trees well protected from wind until established using fine mesh netting. It is worth planting nurse shrubs alongside. Brooms are excellent for the purpose, but they must be removed after about four or five years to avoid overcrowding. By this time the golden rain tree should be growing away nicely. Special pruning is not normally required, apart from removing feathers from the trunk and cutting out suckers.

Propagation Sow seeds in containers during autumn or early spring. Chill for six to eight weeks before bringing into warmth to germinate at 60°F (16°C). Prick out singly into small pots using a good soil-based potting compost. Harden off and stand outdoors. Grow on for two or three years, overwintering under cover.

Problems Unlikely.

Laburnum x Watereri 'Vossii'

Golden Chain, Laburnum
Hardiness HRI
Deciduous tree

Description A highly popular and widely planted small to medium-sized tree; ht to 15ft (4.5m). Habit is variable – ranging from rounded or spreading to vase-shaped with a wide top. Without doubt the main attribute lies in the bright yellow pendulous masses of pea-like flowers during May and June. In late summer, poisonous green seedpods turn to brown and should be gathered if young children play in the garden. The bark of young wood is glossy and green and persists through winter. *L.* 'Vossii' is generally considered to be one of the best, if not the best, laburnum for garden display.

Fig 75 The ever popular laburnum, with its pendulous yellow racemes is a familiar sight in late spring – it grows well in most soils and situations.

Varieties The following varieties, if not quite up to the high standards of *L.* 'Vossii', are none the less excellent and garden worthy. *L.alpinum* 'Pendulum', the weeping scotch laburnum; ht to 15ft (4.5m) – slow-growing with long golden tassels. *L.anagyroides*, the common laburnum; ht to 15ft (4.5m) – flowers a fortnight earlier than *L.* 'Vossii' with golden tassels somewhat shorter than most other varieties. *L.a.* 'Aureum' – a golden-leaved form of the common laburnum.

Position and use Flowering is more prolific in sun. But light partial shade is no serious detriment to growth; in fact, foliage colour is likely to be fresher. Although laburnums are very hardy and stand up to wind as well as or better than most trees, avoid extreme exposure to gale-force winds by careful siting. In view of the

poisonous seedpods, avoid planting in reach of young children.

Provided it is of average fertility and reasonable depth, any free-draining garden soil, including chalk, should suffice. Improve heavy wet clay soils before planting.

Laburnums are fairly versatile, being suitable for use: as single specimens; in shrub borders; in hedgerows; as wall and arbour trees; in containers.

Treatment Plant out during autumn or spring, preferably using container-raised stock. Plant up containers in spring. Stake and tie securely for the first few years until established and rootfirm – vital in exposed sites. No special pruning is needed beyond cutting out deadwood, weak and misplaced shoots in autumn or winter.

Propagation Raise common laburnum from seed sown in autumn and chilled under a frame. Bring into warmth in late winter and germinate at 60°F (16°C). Prick out, harden off, and grow on until autumn when they should be ready for planting out. Graft named varieties on to common laburnum rootstocks in spring. Grow on for two years and plant out in autumn.

Problems On occasions the blotch miner disfigures the foliage. In bad attacks, spray with insecticide.

Liquidambar Styraciflua

Sweet Gum
Hardiness HR3
Deciduous tree

Description A medium to large tree; ht to 20ft (6m) and more. Normally grown as a standard, sweet gum is conical when young and becomes dome-shaped as it matures. This is a fine foliage tree with glossy green maple-like leaves which turn to brilliant shades of crimson, red, purple and gold in autumn. In winter the silvery-grey bark is an added attraction. The yellow spring flowers are somewhat inconspicuous.

Varieties Although *L.styraciflua* is the variety usually seen, there are some uncommon forms worth searching out; they may not be readily available. *L.formosana monticola*, ht to 17ft (5m) or more – pink and red spring foliage turns through green and back to red again in autumn. Only plant in the most favoured gardens. *L.styraciflua* 'Aureum'; ht to 20ft (6m) – the variegated yellow and green summer foliage turns to crimson and gold in autumn. *L.s.* 'Variegata'; ht to 20ft (6m) – the creamy-white-margined green leaves of late spring and summer take on pink shades in late summer and autumn.

Position and use A sunny spot is best. But shade for part of the day is acceptable. Reserve sweet gum for sheltered situations which preferably have a south or west aspect.

Autumn colouring is best on lime-free to near neutral soils. The soil should be deep, moist, fertile and free draining. But avoid planting in over-rich soils, which will result in some loss of colour.

All the varieties listed make spectacular specimens in grass, but tend to grow rather large for small gardens. Here they are best grown and retrained in containers, where they look very attractive.

Treatment Buy container-raised stock and plant in autumn or spring – no matter whether in open ground or in containers. Use lime-free soil-based mixtures in containers. To encourage compactness and to overcome any tendency to sparse branching, shorten back new growths by a half to one-third each autumn for the first two or three years after planting. Subsequently, no special treatment should be necessary.

Propagation Sow *L.styraciflua*, in autumn in containers under a frame. Germination is slow and can take up to two years. Pot up singly and grow on for two or three years – overwintering under cover – before planting out.

Named varieties are best layered in autumn. Rooted layers should be ready to sever, lift and plant out in two years. Alternatively, graft named varieties on to seedling rootstocks in spring.

Problems Unlikely.

Magnolia x Soulangiana

Magnolia
Hardiness HR2
Deciduous tree or shrub

Description A very popular small tree of spreading habit and exotic appearance; ht to 12ft (3.5m). Normally grown as a basal branching bush with a single short trunk. It may also be grown as a multi-stemmed shrub. The spectacular tinged purple-white flowers are large and tulip-like as they open during April. They continue in succession through into May. The large glossy leaves are quite decorative during summer.

Fig 76 Magnolia produces spectacular flowers.

Varieties *M.grandiflora* 'Exmouth'; ht to 18ft (5m) – make an eye-catching evergreen wall tree or shrub. Large white flowers keep up a succession of bloom from July to September. Large glossy leaves give year-round interest. *M.kobus*; ht to 12ft (3.5m) and more – makes an attractive small to medium-sized deciduous tree, producing white flowers in April and May. But slow to start blooming – flowers are rare on trees under ten to twelve years old. *M.* x *soulangiana* 'Lennei'; ht to 12ft (3.5m) – forms a wide-spreading small deciduous tree which flowers in April and May. The extra large rose-purple blooms have a creamy-purple flush inside the flower petals.

Position and use Reserve magnolias for warm, sunny situations – preferably with a south or west-facing aspect. Avoid east-facing sites at all costs. Rapid thawing will destroy buds and flowers. Magnolias also need to be sheltered from cold and drying spring winds.

Lime-free, well-drained, medium loam, well-enriched with peat or leaf mould, spells excellence. *M.grandiflora* and *M.kobus* can tolerate some lime content in the soil.

All magnolias make fine specimens in grass and hard-surfaced areas, but *M.grandiflora* needs wall protection. They do well in containers.

Treatment Buy container-raised trees and plant out during spring into well-prepared ground or containers. Stake and tie. Mulch with peat in the first and subsequent springs. In addition, for the first two to three winters protect the roots from frost with a deep layer of straw or leaves. Restrict pruning to the minimum to keep trees in shape. On wall-trained trees cut out shoots which grow straight out from the wall at right angles.

Propagation Layer in late autumn or spring by pinning down young ripewood within easy reach of the ground. Rooted layers should be ready to sever from the parent tree, lift and replant within about two years of pegging down.

Alternatively, take 4in (10cm) semi-ripewood cuttings in July. Root in warmth at 70°F (21°C).

Pot up singly and overwinter indoors. Harden off in spring and grow on for two or three years, giving frost protection each winter.

Problems Be vigilant for chlorosis (leaf yellowing) – likely with some varieties when grown on chalk soils. See page 78.

Malus Sylvestris

Apple
Hardiness HR2
Deciduous tree

Description Apple trees are extremely variable in shape and size depending upon variety, rootstock, soil and site, as well as method of training. Height ranges from about 7ft (2m) for miniature bush and cordons to approx 17ft (5m) for large bush and half-standards. Trees grown as bush and half-standards are normally rounded or spreading in habit. Their pink and white spring flowers are the main decorative feature – with the bonus of gold, red, crimson or green dessert and culinary fruits in summer and autumn.

Fig 77 Malus, *the apple tree is both attractive and useful.*

Varieties There is little to choose between varieties with regard to the decorative value of flowers. The main differences lie between dessert and culinary varieties; and in fruit colour and season of harvest.

Dessert apples in order of ripening: 'Discovery' – crimson and yellow fruits ripen in summer. 'James Grieve' – pale yellow, streaked crimson fruits ready late autumn. 'Lord Lambourne' – green flushed-red fruits ready late autumn. 'Cox's Orange Pippin' – greenish yellow or yellow suffused red, ripens late autumn and winter.

Culinary apples in order of ripening: 'Arthur Turner' – golden yellow with orange flush, ready late summer to early autumn. 'Bramley's Seedling' – green and red fruits are ready late autumn and winter.

Position and use Grow in sun or partial shade. In general, dessert varieties need more sun than culinary. Sheltered, warm sites, protected from cold north and easterly spring winds, with freedom from late spring frosts are ideal. South and west-facing aspects – including walls – are best. Warmth and shelter help to ensure good pollination at blossom time.

Any reasonably fertile and free-draining garden soil – including chalk provided it is not too shallow – should support apples.

Apples make attractive free-standing and wall specimens; are useful for screening when trained as cordons, espaliers and fans; and are effective in containers.

Treatment Plant out in autumn and early winter – allowing 3ft (1m) between cordons; 7ft (2m) between miniature bush; 12ft (3.5m) between large bush, espalier and fan; and 15ft (4.5m) between half-standards. Ensure that trees grown for fruit are either self-fertile, family trees, or have a suitable pollinator variety growing nearby. Summer prune wall-trained trees. See page 00.

Propagation Bud in July or graft in March on to selected rootstocks. Use M25 for big trees; MM106 for semi-dwarfing; M26 for dwarf; and M27 for very small or miniature trees.

Propagating from seed is a fun thing only – results are uncertain. Sow in autumn or spring, under cover in slight warmth.

Problems Look out for aphid, caterpillar and red spider. Also apple canker, mildew and scab. See Chapter 8.

Malus 'John Downie'

Crab Apple
Hardiness HRI
Deciduous tree

Description A first class small to medium-sized tree; ht to about 17–20ft (5–6m). Conical habit when young, spreading with age. In spring pink buds are freely produced – opening out into white flowers. During the summer and early autumn the ripening fruits turn an attractive orange scarlet.

Varieties The following selection of choice flowering crabs grow to about 17–20ft (5–6m) – except where stated otherwise. *M.floribunda*, Japanese crab – of rounded habit with red spring buds, pink flowers and cherry red autumn fruits. *M.* 'Golden Hornet' – of conical habit becoming rounded; white-flowered in spring, green summer foliage and yellow autumn fruits. *M.* 'Lemoinei' – rounded habit becoming spreading; crimson spring flowers, purple summer foliage and red autumn fruits make it most colourful. *M.* 'Profusion' – of spreading or rounded habit; coppery crimson spring leaves, purplish red spring flowers and red autumn fruits. *M.sargentii*; ht to 10ft (3m) – of rounded habit; scented white spring flowers, green leaves, and small bright red autumn fruits.

Position and use Crabs do well in sun and partial shade. But the foliage colour of purple and crimson-leaved varieties is much improved in sun. Although they can tolerate reasonable exposure to wind, crabs fruit much better when sheltered from cold north and east spring winds.

Any average garden soil of moderate fertility will suit.

Use crabs as specimen trees in lawns, grass, verges and hard-standing areas; among shrubs; in containers.

Treatment Plant out in autumn or spring, preferable using container-raised stock – but strongly recommended for setting out in spring. Plant up containers in spring. Shorten back weak, crossing and inward growing branchlets during autumn and winter. Take out misplaced shoots and deadwood at the same time.

Propagation The varieties listed can be budded in July or grafted in March – on to either seedling crab rootstock or selected apple rootstocks.

To propagate from seed, for fun and for rootstocks, sow in autumn and chill. Germinate in warmth during spring at 60°F (16°C). Prick out into small pots and grow on.

Problems As for apple.

Morus Nigra

Mulberry
Hardiness HR2
Deciduous tree

Description A small to medium-sized, slow-growing tree of character; ht to 17ft (5m) and more. A rounded or spreading dense crown of branches is typical. Usually grown as a bush tree or short standard on a gnarled trunk. Long lived. Noted for its large, dark green leaves. The flowers are inconspicuous. They are followed by raspberry-like edible fruits which turn from orange-scarlet through to purple as they ripen during August and September.

Varieties The closely related white mulberry, *M.alba*, reaches a similar size to *M.nigra* – but is

Fig 78 The mulberry, Morus nigra, is slow growing but ultimately forms a small tree of great character, producing raspberry-like fruits when mature.

quicker growing and produces creamy white fruits which ripen to pink. *M.a.* 'Pendula' is a slightly slower-growing weeping form.

Position and use A warm, sunny site is essential for fruiting. Plant in a sheltered situation protected from cold north and east winds. In cool northern gardens grow on a sunny south-facing wall.

Aim to provide a deep, moist but well-drained, medium loam.

In warm sheltered gardens, grow as a specimen tree in grass, avoid planting in/near hard-surfaced areas where the fruits are likely to cause staining.

Treatment Plant out in autumn – never in spring, because of the risk of the severe bleeding to which mulberries are highly prone. Keep pruning to a minimum, carrying out any that is necessary during autumn. Again, this is to avoid possible bleeding.

Propagation Take 5–6in (12–15cm) semi-ripewood cuttings in July. They root easily under a shaded frame or indoors. Pot up and grow on for two or three years, giving winter protection. Alternatively, 12in (30cm) hardwood cuttings taken in November will normally root within twelve months – outdoors in a sheltered corner or under a shaded frame.

Problems Normally little troubled by pest or disease. But netting against birds is vital as the fruits ripen.

Parrotia Persica

Persian Ironwood
Hardiness HR3
Deciduous tree

Description Normally makes a small to medium-sized tree, ht to 17ft (5m). But in good conditions can grow considerably larger to 25ft (75m). Is of a wide, spreading habit. Autumn foliage is outstanding. The large, beech-like green summer leaves turn to brilliant crimson, gold, orange and red shades before leaf fall. Another attribute is the red flower tufts which appear on bare branches – normally between February and April. Also, the grey flaking bark which creates a patchwork effect in grey and pink is most pleasing.

Varieties Only one noteworthy garden variety seems to be in general cultivation, namely *Pp.*'Pendula'; ht to 15ft (4.5m) – an attractive weeping dome-shaped form of Persian ironwood. It has splendid autumn tints and red spring flowers.

Position and use Although partial shade is tolerated, plant in full sun for maximum autumn colouring. A warm, sheltered situation is desirable, with a south or west-facing aspect. Avoid east-facing sites, especially those exposed to early morning sun where a quick thaw would spell the ruination of spring flowers.

Fig 79 Parrotia – *its autumn foliage is outstanding.*

A free-draining, moisture-retentive, fertile medium loam is needed for best results – preferably on the acid side.

Persian ironwood makes: a good specimen in lawn or hard-surfaced area; a satisfactory wall tree; a useful shrubbery tree; and a sound container tree.

Treatment Buy container-raised trees and set out in autumn or spring. Plant up containers in spring. Minimal pruning is required beyond shortening back branches in autumn, to shape the tree.

Propagation Layering is the easiest way to propagate Persian ironwood. In autumn, peg down layers of young wood within reach of the ground. Rooted layers should be ready for lifting in about two years.

Alternatively, graft *Pp.* 'Pendula' on to seedling or layered rootstocks in March.

The original *P.persica* can be raised from seed sown in autumn under a cold frame. Germination may take eighteen months. Pot up as soon as seedlings show and grow on for a few years.

Problems Nothing serious is likely.

Prunus 'Pendula Rosea'

Weeping Cherry
Cheal's Weeping Cherry
Hardiness HR2
Deciduous tree

Description An attractive dome-shaped small tree; ht about 10ft (3m). Normally grown as a weeping standard. The main feature is the annual display of pink buds which open to double flowers of bright rose pink, seen cascading down the branches during March and April. Bright green leaves provide a pleasing foil to the flowers.

Varieties From the immense range of flowering cherries is a short selection of the choicest for smaller gardens: *P.* 'Amanogawa', the Lombardy poplar cherry; ht to 17ft (5m). Very narrow and columnar in habit. Pale pink flowers in April and May. *P.* 'Kanzan'; ht to 23ft (7m). A vase-like wide-topped habit. Very popular. Double pink May flowers. Leaves open bronze, turn green in summer and gold, pink and red in autumn. *P.* 'Pendula Rubra' – size and habit as *p.* 'Pendula Rosea'. Flowers are single and rose pink. *P.* × *sargentii*; ht about 20ft (6m). Spreading habit. Single pink flowers open during March and April. Leaves burst bright red, turn green, and then change to red tints again in autumn. *P.subhirtella* 'Autumnalis Rosea'; ht to 17ft (5m). Spreading habit. Pale pink flowers are produced intermittently between autumn and spring. The green leaves of summer turn to red, crimson and bronze in autumn.

Fig 80 Prunus – tree top.

Position and use Aim to plant cherries in an open, sunny situation – preferably one which is not too exposed.

Any free-draining, reasonably deep, fertile garden soil will suffice – including chalk. But preferably nothing too rich, or risk excess leaf at the expense of flowers.

Use as a specimen tree in: lawn, hard-surfaced area, shrub border; and in containers.

Treatment Plant in autumn or spring into open ground. Opt for autumn planting of containers. Minimal pruning is required. Carry out any necessary work during July and August. Wounds heal naturally at this time and the risk of Silver leaf disease is lessened. Don't prune in spring or there is a risk of bleeding. If trees become too vigorous, root prune in late autumn.

Propagation Bud on to selected rootstocks in July. The rootstock normally favoured is F12/I. But for small, dwarf trees of about half the sizes quoted above, try the Colt rootstock. It is showing great promise, but as it may be in short supply for a year or two it may take some finding.

Problems Spray against aphid and caterpillar if they look like getting out of hand.

Prunus Cerasifera 'Pissardii'

Purple-leaved Plum
Hardiness HRI
Deciduous tree

Description A small to medium-sized rounded tree; ht to 23ft (7m). Usually grown as a standard. The main attraction is the foliage. The leaves open a reddish-wine colour, turn to a purple-brown – which is then held throughout summer. White flowers are produced in March and April.

Varieties *P.c.* 'Nigra' is similar in size and habit to *P.c.* 'Pissardii'. Summer leaves and young stems are blackish-purple, pink flowers bloom during

Fig 81 The purple-leaved plum, Prunus cerasifera 'Pissardii' is very hardy and easy to grow in most average soils and sites.

March and April. *P.* 'Trailblazer'; ht to about 17ft (5m). Rounded or spreading habit. Leaves are bronze at first, becoming purple-green during summer. Pinkish buds open to white flowers in March/April. Cherry-red plums follow in August/September. *P. persica* 'Pink Charming'. Flowering peach; ht to 17ft (5m) — rounded, bushy habit. Related to *P.c.* 'Pissardii', but not so hardy (HR3). Bright pink flowers in April are the main feature.

Position and use   A sunny, open situation — not too exposed — should ensure good foliage colour and free flowering. Ornamental plums can tolerate a fair amount of wind, but Flowering Peach needs shelter from the north and east — give it a south or west aspect.

Average garden soils, including chalky, are suitable — given free drainage and average fertility.

Ornamental plums are highly versatile. Use them as specimen trees in grass and hard standing; as focal points among shrubs and ground cover; for hedgerow trees and for screening. Use them in containers.

They are good in towns as well as at the coast. Flowering peach makes a good wall-trained specimen. Otherwise give it warmth and shelter and use as a specimen.

Treatment   Aim to complete all planting during autumn, preferably not in spring when in flower. Little pruning is needed. To obtain a formal, clipped effect, ornamental plums will stand clipping two or three times during summer.

Propagation   Bud on to selected rootstocks in July. Rootstock St Julien 'A' is popular. But try the newer dwarf 'Pixy' rootstocks where smaller trees appeal — of about half the sizes quoted above. Take 4in (10cm) semi-ripewood cuttings of ornamental plum in July. They will root readily under a shaded closed frame — or indoors in an inflated plastic bag.

Problems   Spray against aphid and caterpillar where they threaten.

Prunus Various

Plum and Cherry
Hardiness HR2 and 3
Deciduous trees

Description   Rounded oval and spreading trees of variable size. Until the introduction of dwarfing rootstocks these trees were considered too large for the smaller garden. Nowadays grown as bush trees and short standards. All offer attractive white spring blossom — followed by the familiar edible crops of plum and cherry. Pollination and fruit set problems can be resolved, in part at least, by the use of self-fertile varieties — which set crops with their own pollen.

106

Varieties *Plum*; ht about 10–15ft (3–4.5m) on dwarf rootstocks. 'Czar' – oval habit. Purple rounded fruits in August. Culinary, self-fertile variety. 'Denniston's Superb' – rounded habit. Greenish-golden fruits ready in August. Self-fertile dessert variety. 'Victoria' – rounded or spreading crown. Red and yellow oval fruits ready for dessert or culinary use in September. Self-fertile.

Sweet cherry; ht to about 15ft (4.5m) on dwarf rootstocks. 'Stella' – rounded or spreading habit. The white spring flowers are followed by red dessert cherries in July. Self-fertile.

Position and use Select a sunny situation, sheltered from cold north and east spring winds. A south-facing aspect presents fewest problems. But plums will tolerate a west-facing outlook. Choose varieties like 'Czar' and 'Victoria' for northern gardens.

Deep, moist but well-drained, fertile loams that are neutral or slightly chalky are best.

Grow as free-standing trees in grass – or train fanwise against a wall. Will give reasonable results grown in containers.

Treatment All planting is best completed in autumn. When grown as a free-standing form, minimal pruning is needed. Summer prune and train wall forms, see page 69. Any over-vigorous, unproductive trees should be root pruned in the winter.

Propagation Bud all the varieties listed here in July – on to selected rootstocks. Use the dwarf 'Pixy' rootstocks for varieties of plum, and the dwarfing 'Colt' rootstocks for the cherry.

Problem Control aphid, caterpillar and red spider with insecticide sprays to safeguard crops.

Pyrus Salicifolia 'Pendula'

Weeping Silver Pear
Hardiness HR2
Deciduous tree

Description A highly ornamental small to medium-sized dome-shaped tree; ht to 20ft (6m). Normally grown as a weeping standard. The silvery, willow-shaped leaves provide interest from spring through to autumn and make an excellent foil for the April blossoms. This is one of the best ornamental pears for a long-term display.

Varieties *P.calleryana* 'Chanticleer' forms a narrowly conical and tapering small to medium-sized tree; ht up to 20ft (6m). In April mature trees are smothered in white blossom. The

Fig 82 Pyrus salicifolia 'Pendula' is a grey-leaved weeping tree of pleasing outline, but needs space to develop.

glossy green summer leaves turn to shades of red and rich wine in autumn. *P.communis* 'Beech Field' is a small tree of columnar habit; ht to 17ft (5m) – with a profusion of white April blossom and autumn leaf tints in orange-yellow. *P.nivalis,* the snow pear, so named because of its silvery white summer foliage. Grows to about 17ft (5m) in height. In April the branches are laden with masses of white flowers.

Position and use Grow ornamental pears in sunny or partially shaded, fairly open situations. But avoid extreme exposure to strong winds.

Any free-draining, ordinary garden soil of average fertility – including chalk – will suffice.

Ornamental pears make excellent specimens in grass verges, lawns and hard-surfaced areas – as well as in containers.

Treatment The ideal time to plant is autumn or early winter – in both open ground and containers. Protect young trees from strong winds until well shaped. Standards need to be firmly staked and tied; pay particular attention to weeping varieties as they can be a bit top heavy. Little pruning is called for except to shorten misplaced, crossing, weak and in-growing shoots – the work is best carried out in autumn.

Propagation Bud in July, or graft in March-April – on to seedling rootstocks of common pear, *Pyrus communis*. Alternatively, for smaller trees, use selected Quince A or C rootstocks.

To raise seedling rootstocks, sow in spring or autumn under a cold frame. Expect germination in about a month. Pot up singly and grow on for two to three years.

Problems If caterpillars are getting a hold, spray with insecticide. Use fungicide against scab.

Rhus Typhina

Stag's Horn Sumach
Hardiness HR2
Deciduous tree or shrub

Description A very desirable small wide-topped tree; ht to about 17ft (5m). Usually grown as a bush tree or short standard. The main feature is the foliage. Large pinnate leaves, green in summer, turn to brilliant shades of flame, gold, orange and red in autumn. The inconspicuous male and female flowers are carried on separate trees. But it is only the female trees which produce eye-catching crimson club-like fruit spikes in autumn and winter. The brown bark of young wood is thickly covered with velvety, reddish-brown hairs. Hence the 'Stag's Horn' derivation.

Variety *R.t.* 'Laciniata' – apart from finely divided leaves which colour up even more vividly, this variety is very similar in size and habit to *R.typhina*. *R.glabra*, the smooth sumach; ht to 10ft (3m) – a smooth-stemmed smaller version of *R.typhina*. *R.trichocarpa*; ht to 17ft (5m) – downy leaves are coppery-pink on opening; they turn through green, and then to orange in autumn.

Position and use Grow in sun for the finest autumn foliage. But even in partial shade it will do well. Tolerant of moist winds typical of coastal areas. But avoid very exposed sites. Plant in any aspect – except north-facing.

Most free-draining, fertile garden soils, including chalk, will suit. Preferably avoid anything too rich.

Stag's horn sumach makes a truly garden-worthy specimen tree for grass, hard-surfaced areas and containers. Good also among shrubs. Does well in towns as well as in coastal areas.

Treatment Plant out in autumn or spring. To avoid a 'thicket' type of growth, remove any suckers at the same time. Subsequently remove all suckers each autumn. Minimal pruning is needed, apart from cutting back any dead wood in autumn or spring. However, it is possible to stimulate the production of extra large leaves by hard pruning in March or April – back almost to ground level.

Propagation The easiest way is gently to detach

rooted suckers in autumn and plant them out in a sheltered position to grow on for a year or so.

Alternatively, take 4–6in (10–15in) semi-ripewood cuttings in July and root under a closed shaded frame, or indoors in an inflated plastic bag and shaded – at about 60–65°F (16–18°C). Pot up when rooted and grow on for twelve months before planting out.

Problems   As a rule nothing serious is likely.

Robinia Pseudoacacia 'Frisia'

Golden False Acacia
Hardiness HR2 and 3
Deciduous tree

Description   A spectacular medium to large rounded tree; ht to about 23ft (7m). Normally grown as a standard. Noted for its outstanding greeny-gold foliage, which persists from spring to autumn – when the leaves take on coppery tints. Clusters of white flowers provide June interest. When in full leaf, the branches and vigorous prickly, spined shoots are inclined to brittleness and breakage in strong winds.

Varieties   R.hispida, the rose acacia; ht to 15ft (4.5m) – has pink flowers in May and June. Best grown as a wall-trained fan. R.pseudoacacia, False Acacia; ht to 30ft (9m) or more – the crown is open textured and rounded. Clusters of white June flowers are typical. R.p. 'Fastigata'; ht to 23ft (7m) – has ascending branches with a narrow columnar outline. Again, white June flowers are a feature. R.p. 'Inermis', the mophead acacia; ht to 17ft (5m) – this is a compact, roundheaded small to medium-sized tree with green foliage. It rarely flowers.

Position and use   A sunny, or partially shaded site will suit most false acacias. R.hispida needs full sun and is at its best against a south or west-facing wall. R.p. 'Inermis' will tolerate more shade than most. In all cases avoid exposed situations or risk branch breakages.

Fig 83   Robinia hispida *(the rose acacia) needs a warm, sunny site if it is to flower freely.*

Any light to medium free-draining average garden soil will suit – including chalky. Either avoid heavy wet soils or set about improving them drastically before planting. False acacia make good specimen trees in grass, hard-surfaced areas, against walls, and in containers.

Treatment   Plant out during autumn or spring – in both open ground and containers. Opt for container-raised stock – and small trees – to minimize root disturbance. Otherwise risk a setback to growth which can be serious with large trees. Those between 3 and 5ft (1 and 1.5m) in height are best for transplanting. Remove basal suckers and cut out dead or damaged wood in autumn – apart from this little pruning is needed.

Propagation Gently detach rooted suckers in late autumn. Plant out in a warm, sheltered spot – or pot up into containers – and grow on out of wind for a year. This is the most reliable method of obtaining trees identical to the parent. Species like *R.hispida* and *R.pseudoacacia* can be successfully raised from seed sown during April – but expect some variation. Germinate under a frame or indoors at 60°F (16°C). Pot up seedlings as soon as big enough to handle. Grow on for another year or two, moving on into larger containers as necessary.

Problems Unlikely.

Salix Caprea 'Kilmarnock'

Kilmarnock Willow
Hardiness HRl
Deciduous tree

Description A small umbrella-shaped tree, with stiffly downswept branches; ht to 10ft (3m). Normally grown as a weeping standard. An excellent willow for small gardens. Male trees carry yellow catkins in late winter/early spring – while silvery catkins are borne on female trees. All trees have silvery foliage from spring through to autumn.

Varieties (weeping) *S. × chrysocoma*, golden weeping willow, makes a large pendulous, broadly dome-shaped tree; ht to 50ft (15m). The yellow-barked young shoots are seen at their best in winter. Unsuited to small gardens. *S.purpurea* 'Pendula', American weeping willow, forms a fairly compact dome; ht to 17ft (5m). The long, slender, purplish stems are covered with blue-green leaves during summer.

Varieties (upright) *S.alba* 'Chermesina', scarlet willow, forms a medium to large columnar tree; ht to 30ft (9m). Grown mainly for its orange-scarlet new winter stems. Summer foliage is a not unattractive yellowish-green. *S.a.* 'Vitellina', golden willow, makes a small to medium-sized tree; ht to 25ft (7.5m) with yellow new wood for winter interest. *S.matsudana* 'Tortuosa', corkscrew willow, makes a medium to large spreading tree, ht to 40ft (12m). This willow carries unusual spiralling stems which are best seen in winter.

Position to use Grow well in sun, partial shade and light permanent shade. Although willows are very hardy it is best to avoid windswept and very exposed sites.

Willows are very adaptable and will thrive in most free-draining soils of average fertility. But they prefer deep, moisture-retentive loams.

Use weeping trees as specimens – in lawns, by the waterside and in hard-surfaced areas. Non-weeping varieties make good waterside trees. They look well among shrubs and are useful for screening.

NOTE: The roots of willow are notorious for damaging drains and building foundations. Plant all willows at a distance from buildings equal to double their ultimate height. Alternatively, use planting boxes. See page 38–9.

Treatment Plant out during autumn and spring. Weeping willows need little pruning beyond keeping in shape and cutting out dead or weak growth in winter. Upright varieties – grown for their bark or stem interest – can be restrained to 10ft (3m) or less, by hard cutting back in March or April. This also promotes the growth of plenty of new wood which is always the most highly coloured.

Propagation Upright varieties: take 10–12in (25–30cm) long cuttings of well-ripened new season's wood in November. Root in a warm sheltered spot outdoors or under a cold frame. Weeping varieties; graft on to *Salix alba*, cutting raised rootstocks in March.

Problems Spray with insecticide to control aphid, caterpillar and scale insects if attacks look like getting out of hand.

Sophora Tetraptera 'Grandiflora'

Kowhai
Hardiness HR3
Semi-evergreen tree

Description A small to medium-sized rounded tree which is best grown against a wall; ht to 17ft (5m). On mature trees, yellow pea-like flowers are carried in April and May. The distinctive zig-zagging branches bear pinnate green leaves.

Varieties *S.japonica*, the pagoda tree, a deciduous rounded tree; ht up to about 20ft (6m). This is the one most frequently grown. On mature trees, pendulous clusters of white mini wisteria-like flowers open during September. *S.j.* 'Pendula'; ht 17ft (5m). Is of dome-shaped weeping habit – otherwise similar to the pagoda tree. *S.microphylla* is similar in size and habit to *S.t.* 'Grandiflora' – but is slower growing, has wiry branches and smaller leaflets.

Position and use These trees do best in a warm, sunny situation – sheltered from cold north and east winds. Against a sunny south or west-facing wall is first class. Avoid east-facing walls or there is a risk of scorching and blackening, due to early morning sun thawing out frozen leaves and buds too quickly.

A warm, well-drained, fertile soil will suit. Use all varieties mentioned as specimen wall trees. They are also suitable for containers.

Treatment Aim to complete all planting during April and May using container-raised stock. Minimal pruning is required beyond shaping trees and cutting out dead shoots – work which is best carried out during summer. Container trees may need pinching two or three times during summer.

Propagation Sow in containers during spring and germinate indoors in warmth at 60°F (16°C). Prick out singly into small pots and grow on for three to four years before planting out – standing outdoors during the summer months and protecting during winter. Graft *S.j.* 'Pendula' on to seedling rootstocks in April.

Problems Following a severe winter, look for dieback at branch tips. Check by cutting back to sound wood in late spring.

Sorbus Aria 'Lutescens'

Whitebeam
Hardiness HRI
Deciduous tree

Description A valuable small to medium-sized tree of conical habit, broadening out with age; ht to 25ft (7.5m). Usually grown as a standard. As they burst the leaves are grey-white – as the season advances they show green on the upper surface with a grey reverse. A characteristic display of white flower clusters would be from late May to July – followed by masses of red autumn berries.

Fig 84 Sorbus aria flowers from late May to July.

Varieties *S.aria* make an attractive small to medium rounded tree; ht to about 23ft (7m). The grey-white spring leaves turn through green to a dull red and gold in autumn. Flowers and berries as *S.a.* 'Lutescens'. *S.* × *hostii*, is a very useful small tree; ht to 13ft (4m). The green summer leaves with their grey-white undersurface provide an attractive foil for the pink May flowers and the orange-red autumn berries. *S.folgneri,* a small to medium-sized broadly oval good tree; ht to 20ft (6m). The dark green leaves have a white downy reverse. In autumn the upper surfaces turn to shades of crimson, orange and scarlet. Flowers and berries as for *S.a.* 'Lutescens'.

Position and use Set out whitebeams in a sunny or partially shaded, open situation. These are hardy trees and will stand a fair amount of wind.

Fig 85 The mountain ash, Sorbus aucuparia, *is a hardy and reliable tree – equally at home in town or country.*

Any reasonably fertile, free-draining garden soil should suit – including chalky.

Whitebeams are good as specimens in lawns, verges and hardstanding areas. They look well among shrubs, in hedgerows and containers. Suitable for towns and for planting at the coast.

Treatment Plant out into open ground and into containers during autumn or spring. Little pruning is needed apart from cutting out weak growths and deadwood in autumn or winter.

Propagation In the case of named varieties – bud in July or graft in March. Work on to seedling rootstocks of *S.aria*.

To raise rootstocks sow *S.aria* in autumn under a cold frame to chill. Bring into warmth to germinate at 60°F (16°C). Pot up singly and grow on for two or three years.

Problems If caterpillars become a nuisance, spray with insecticide.

Sorbus Aucuparia

Mountain Ash, Rowan
Hardiness HRI
Deciduous tree

Description A small to medium-sized oval or round-headed tree; ht to 23ft (7m). Usually grown as a standard. Leaves, pinnate, ash-like and green, turn to red and yellow in autumn. The clusters of slightly scented white flowers of May/June are followed by yellow berries in July. These turn red from August onwards and are carried through into autumn. Mountain ash is reliable and hardy in most places in the British Isles.

Varieties *S.a.* 'Asplenifolia' makes an oval-headed tree of similar size to *S.aucuparia*. Flowers and berries are similar, too. *S.a.* 'Xanthocarpa' apart from being yellow berrying is similar to *S.aucuparia*. *S.cashmiriana* is conical in habit; ht about 17ft (5m). Pinnate green leaves turn through tints of red in autumn. Pink flowers open in May – to be followed in late summer by clusters of pink-flushed white berries. *S.commixta* is narrow columnar in habit; ht 23ft (7m). The pinnate leaves are copper tinted in spring, turn through green in summer to tints of purple and scarlet in autumn. Flowers and berries as *S.aucuparia*. *S.* 'Joseph Rock' makes a fine columnar tree; ht 27ft (8m), with yellow autumn berries. *S.sargentiana* forms a round, bushy tree; ht about 15ft (4.5m). The green summer foliage turns to bright vermilion in autumn and sets off the clusters of orange-scarlet berries. A good variety for the smaller garden.

Position and use Mountain ash prefer a sunny, open site, but will adapt to partial shade. They stand up well to wind.

Any reasonably fertile, average garden soil will suffice. But avoid planting on very shallow soil overlying chalk – improve beforehand otherwise trees are likely to be shortlived. Mountain ash stands drought better than most.

The varieties mentioned are very versatile. They make excellent specimens in lawns, verges, hard-surfaced areas and containers. They are good in the shrubbery and hedgerow.

Treatment As for whitebeam *S.aria*.

Propagation Bud named varieties in July, or graft in March – on to seedling *S.aucuparia* rootstocks.

To raise rootstocks sow *S.aucuparia* in autumn under a cold frame and treat as whitebeam *S.aria*.

Problems Keep caterpillars in check with insecticide sprays. Use fungicide sprays against outbreaks of rust disease.

Syringa Vulgaris

Lilac
Hardiness HR2
Deciduous tree or shrub

Fig 86 Lilac (Syringa) is noted for its sweetly scented flowers – they provide a relatively short but glorious burst of bloom.

Description A highly popular small tree, usually of upright ascending habit; ht about 10–13ft (3–4m). Normally grown as a bush tree or short standard. The prime attraction is the often spectacular display of sweetly scented flowers between early May and mid-June. A lot depends on variety and local conditions. The flowers are carried in clusters/panicles and may be single, double or semi-double and variously coloured – according to variety. Unfortunately, the flowering season is fairly short – usually no more than three to four weeks. The dull green, heart-shaped leaves are rather uninspiring for the rest of the season. However, they can provide a useful backdrop for other flowering plants. Lilac will adapt well to town and coastal sites.

Varieties The following are of similar size and habit to *S.vulgaris*: 'Charles Joly' – a fine double flowered purple-red. 'Firmament' – a pleasing sky-blue, single flowered. 'Madame Lemoine' – a particularly good double flowered white. 'Maud Notcutt' – an excellent heavy-scented single white which lasts well in water. 'Sensation' – an eye-catching bicolour, white-edged purple, single flowered. 'Souvenir de L.Spath' – an excellent wine-red single.

Position and use Flowering is freer and trees more compact in sunny, fairly open situations than when grown in partial shade.

Lilac thrives on medium to heavy free-draining fertile loams – including those with a high percentage of chalk.

Use as specimens in lawns, verges, hardstanding and containers. Effective in groups or singly among shrubs. Also singly in the hedgerow. They make a useful screen.

Treatment Carry out all planting during spring or autumn. In the first year after planting, remove the flower spikes from young trees when still in bud and before colouring. Subsequently deadhead – important during the second and third years at least to conserve energy. Remove suckers as they arise. Little pruning is needed beyond cutting out deadwood and weak shoots in autumn.

Propagation Most of the varieties mentioned can be increased from 4in (10cm) long semi-ripewood cuttings in July. Root in warmth at 60°F (16°C). But be prepared for a low success rate (10–15 per cent) unless very carefully nursed along. Use proprietary rooting preparation.

Otherwise graft on to privet – *Ligustrum ovalifolum* rootstocks in March.

Problems Spray with insecticide if leaf miner is troublesome.

Tamarix Gallica

Common Tamarisk
Hardiness HR2
Deciduous tree or shrub

Description An attractive small tree of spreading habit; ht to 12ft (3.5m). Usually grown in bush form with basal branching. Attractive slender cylindrical racemes or plume-like arrangements of pink flowers are in evidence from July to September, and are set off by feathery sea-green foliage. An excellent coastal tree.

Varieties *T.parviflora* makes a small bushy spreading tree; ht to 10ft (3m). Deep pink flowers are spectacular during May – arising from bright green feathery foliage. *T. pentandra* is similar in size, shape and habit to *T.gallica* and produces rose-pink tapering racemes at the tips of new season's growths during August and September. The foliage is a feathery blue-green. Less wind resistant than the others. *T.p* 'Rubra' is a deeper-coloured form of *T.pentandra*.

Position and uses Tamarisk grows best in a sunny, open situation – but will tolerate partial shade if not too intense. Once windfirm will stand coastal and even inland breezes. Give *T.pentandra* protection from gale force winds.

Ordinary well-drained fertile garden soil in the light to medium loam range will suit well. Avoid planting on shallow chalky soils.

Use tamarisk as specimens in grass verges, lawns and hard-surfaced areas. Also, effective in groups among shrubs and in grass. They make a good screen – against wind and for privacy.

Treatment Plant during mild spells in autumn or spring. Give wind protection and stake securely for the first season at least – until established and windfirm. Prune *T.parviflora* as soon as flowering finishes in late May – thinning out weak-flowered growth. Flowers are produced on shoots formed the previous year. *T.gallica*, *T.pentandra* and *T.p.* 'Rubra' are pruned in late winter – about

February, so that all spent flower plumes are removed.

Propagation   Take 4–5in (10–12cm) long semi-ripewood cuttings in July. Root indoors at 60°F (16°C). Pot up singly and grow on for a year – overwintering under cover.

Problems   Unlikely.

Trachycarpus Fortunei

Chusan Palm
Hardiness HR3
Evergreen tree

Description   A very distinctive, slow-growing, usually small tree; ht to about 15ft (4.5m). In mild climate areas in south-western districts trees of

Fig 87 Trachycarpus fortunei, *the Chusan palm, is a small tree of great character, but is reliably hardy only in mild climate areas.*

30ft (9m) are not unknown. A cylindrical, thick trunk, covered with dark fibres – the remains of leaf bases – is normal. Topping the trunk is usually a cluster arrangement of 3½ft (1m) wide glossy green, fan-shaped leaves on long stalks. The leaves are a special feature. Arising from the leafstalk bases of female trees come masses of small yellow flowers in May and June. During long, warm summers – which are not all that frequent – black marble-sized fruits are produced as a bonus.

This is the only reliably hardy palm normally grown in the British Isles and is perfect for tropical effects.

Position and use   A warm and sunny – or partially shaded – site is a prerequisite for growing Chusan palm. The warmer the site the bigger the tree will grow. Protection from strong and cold winds – especially those from the north and east – is vital. So, choose a south or west-facing sheltered aspect.

A deep, rich, fertile moist loam, that is free draining and containing plenty of organic matter is required for success.

Chusan palm makes an unusual specimen tree in a lawn or bed – in a walled or enclosed garden. Suitable also for container growing in a courtyard.

Treatment   Plant out container-raised, well-hardened off, biggish trees, during mild weather in April or May. Being slow growing, trees need to be a reasonable size – 5ft (1.5m) or so – before they make any appreciable impact. Protect trees from cold wind with such as netting. Guard against frost damage – especially at the roots – by covering them with a generous layer of straw or leaves for the first few years. Pruning is minimal, consisting of cutting out the odd old, dead or damaged leaf – close to the trunk – in late spring.

Propagation   The easy way is carefully to remove rooted suckers in April or May. Pot them up into 5–6in (13–15cm) pots. Grow on indoors in light, airy conditions at 55–60°F (13–15°C) for three to five years. Shade from strong summer sun and pot on in spring as necessary.

Alternatively, sow seed in warmth at 75°F (23°C). Prick out singly into small pots and grow on indoors as for rooted suckers.

Problems Outdoors few difficulties are experienced. Be on guard against red spider and scale indoors.

Fig 88   An attractive conifer shrub grouping.

CONIFERS

Abies Koreana

Korean Fir
Hardiness HR2
Evergreen conifer

Description A small, slow-growing conifer; ht to about 10ft (3m), but often no more than 7ft (2m). Usually of basal branching conical habit. The leaves are needle-like short and flat; glossy dark green on the upper surface with white reverse – providing year-round foliage interest.

Eye-catching, blue cylindrical cones are carried on quite young trees, usually of seven years and less.

Varieties *A.k.* 'Aurea' is similar to *A.koreana* in habit, but even slower growing. It has pleasing golden-yellow foliage all year – very pronounced in winter. *A.k.* 'Horstmann's Silberlocke' is of slow-growing habit with upturned leaves showing the white undersides of the needles.

Position and use To ensure good foliage colour and cone production aim to plant in full sun. However, partial shade will be tolerated. Avoid exposed, windswept sites, preferably selecting a south or west aspect. Avoid east-facing sites where frozen foliage and scorch are likely.

Fig 89   Abies koreana.

Any reasonably fertile free-draining soil should suffice. Avoid planting on chalky soils.

These firs are all very useful for planting as single specimens or groups in the rock garden, island beds, lawns, hard-surfaced areas and containers.

Treatment   Carry out all planting in the ground and in containers during mild weather in autumn or spring. Buy container-raised trees, otherwise risk a setback to growth. Protect from cold, drying winds in the first two winters. In exposed gardens use proprietary anti-wilt preparations. Don't allow young trees to dry out at any time. Pruning needs are minimal – apart from cutting out dead or damaged branches in late spring. However, if forking occurs at the top, take steps to limit to one main leader, by cutting out the weakest or most poorly placed shoot in late spring.

Propagation   Graft named varieties in March, under cover, using *A.koreana* as rootstocks.

For rootstocks or growing on sow *A.koreana* in late autumn or winter. Chill for six to eight weeks, then bring into warmth to germinate at 60°F (16°C). Prick out singly and grow on for three to four years before 'working' or planting out.

Problems   Nothing serious is likely.

Araucaria Araucana

Monkey Puzzle, Chile Pine
Hardiness HRI and 2
Evergreen conifer

Description   A medium to large tree; ht up to about 25ft (7.5m) under average conditions – but it can double this size in favourable, milder areas. A conical or round-headed open habit is typical, becoming domed with age as the lower branches sweep down to the ground. A most distinctive tree of considerable character. Glossy, dark green spiky leaves are arranged spirally

Fig 90   Araucaria araucana.

around the branches which radiate out in whorls from the main trunk. Remarkably hardy for a conifer and will survive town conditions.

Variety   *A. heterophylla*, the Norfolk Island pine is the only close relative of the monkey puzzle in cultivation. Since it is too tender to grow outdoors in this country it is used as a foliage houseplant.

Position and use   Choose a sunny, open situation. Or, at second best, settle for one that is shaded for part of the day only. A south or west-facing aspect, protected from north and east cold winds is desirable, but in no way essential.

117

A fairly deep and fertile, free-draining soil – preferably neither too shallow nor too rich in lime – is the ideal.

Use a monkey puzzle as a specimen on its own in a lawn or grass area. Reserve for medium to large gardens.

Treatment When planting always seek out container-grown stock of not more than 12in (30cm) in height. Plant out in October–November in mild districts and where the soil is light to medium. In cooler areas, in cold gardens and wet districts – as well as on heavy soils – delay planting until spring, in April. Protect against wind for the first two or three winters. Pruning is negligible.

Propagation Sow in a cold frame in March. Prick out singly into small pots and grow on for about four years.

Alternatively take 4in (10cm) tip cuttings in July. Root in warmth at 60–65°F (16–18°C). Pot up singly when rooted and grow on as for seedlings.

Problems Anticipate no serious difficulties.

Calocedrus Decurrens (Libocedrus)

Incense Cedar
Hardiness HR2
Evergreen conifer

Description A medium to large tree of slender, columnar proportions; ht to 27ft (8m). Listed in some catalogues as *Libocedrus decurrens*. The foliage, which is one of the main attractions, is made up of large fan-like sprays of rich green. Even on old trees the leaves are retained down to ground level. The narrow, column-like habit offers quite an appeal of its own – as an architectural plant to frame views.

Varieties The following varieties are somewhat uncommon, and not readily available at garden centres. They are worth searching out from

Fig 91 The narrow columnar outline of the incense cedar (Calocedrus decurrens) *makes this an effective and distinctive accent tree.*

specialist growers. *C.d.* 'Aureovariegata' – similar to *C. decurrens*, but smaller; ht to about 23ft (7m). The rich green leaves have a golden variegation, *C.d.* 'Berrima Gold' makes a columnar tree with domed top. Is similar in height, but wider, than *C.d.* 'Aureovariegata'. The foliage is pale gold, tipped with pink in spring, turning to yellow-green and bronze in winter. The bark is an attractive orange-brown. *C.d.* 'Nana' makes a slow-growing small columnar tree; ht 5ft (1.5m). Foliage similar to *C.decurrens*.

Position and use Select a sunny, warm position. This is important for coloured varieties. *C.decurrens* will stand partial shade. Plant in south or west-facing positions.

A deep moisture-retentive, but free-draining medium loam that is fertile and not excessively chalky should be the aim.

Use incense cedars as single specimens in grass. Or in pairs to frame entrances and the like. The smaller varieties are good in containers and for the rock garden.

Treatment Seek out container-raised trees of 2ft (60cm) or less. Aim to complete all planting in spring – certainly in cool sites. Protect from strong, cold winds or there is a risk of scorching. Little pruning is needed, other than trimming to shape where necessary in spring. If forking occurs, limit to a single leader as with *Abies koreana*.

Propagation Sow *C.decurrens* in containers during October and chill under a cold frame. Move into warmth in late winter to germinate at 60°F (16°C). Pot up singly and grow on for three to four years before planting out.

The varieties mentioned do not come true from seed. Take 3in (8cm) tip cuttings between July and September. Root in warmth at 60–65°F (16–18°C). Pot up when rooted and grow on as for cuttings.

Problems Normally there are no serious difficulties.

Chamaecyparis Lawsoniana 'Ellwoodii'

Cypress
Hardiness HRI
Evergreen conifer

Description An attractive and very popular small to medium-sized slow-growing tree – of columnar single or multi-stem habit; ht 12–15ft (3.5–4m). It normally reaches a height of about 7ft (2m) in ten years, and is very slow growing after that. The foliage is retained well on basal branches to ground level. The leaves are feathery, dark green all year round, and arranged in flattish sprays. Cones are small, pea sized, freely produced and green – turning brown when ripe.

Varieties *C.lawsoniana* varieties are very variable in shape, size and growth rate. The following heights are for conifers ten years after planting out average-sized stock. *C.l.* 'Columnaris Glauca'; ht 12ft (3.5m) – narrow columnar habit with grey-green foliage. *C.l.* 'Ellwoods Gold'; ht 5ft (1.5m) – columnar with gold-tipped branchlets. *C.l.* 'Minima Aurea'; ht 20in (50cm) – compact and pyramidal with golden foliage. *C.l.* 'Minima Glauca'; ht 15in (38cm) – compact, globose habit with bluish-green foliage. *C.l.* 'Lanei Aurea'; ht 7ft (2m) – conical outline with dense golden foliage. *C.l.* 'Pembury Blue'; ht 7ft (2m) – conical with striking silver-blue foliage.

Position and use All varieties do well in sun – but most especially the gold and blue-foliaged kinds. Green and grey-leaved cypress adapt well to partial shade. Golden varieties benefit from some shelter against freezing easterly spring winds.

Fig 92 Chamaecyparis lawsoniana *'Ellwoodii' is a reliable slow-growing conifer. It adapts to most soils and is useful in the small garden.*

Any well-drained garden of average fertility is suitable – including chalky. But avoid extremes of dryness or waterlogging by improving the soil prior to planting.

The cypress mentioned here have many roles ranging from single specimens or groupings in grass, hard-surfaced areas, rock gardens or raised beds. Also planting in containers. Useful for screening.

Treatment Buy small container-raised conifers of not more than 2ft (60cm). Plant out in autumn in mild areas on light soils. Hold back until spring in cold districts and on heavy soils. Treat with anti-wilt preparation in exposed gardens. Protect newly planted cypress against cold, drying winds for the first winter or two. Little pruning is needed apart from shaping trees in late spring if necessary – and correcting forking – see *Abies koreana*, page 116.

Fig 93 A mild climate and moist, acid soil are needed to grow Cryptomeria japonica 'Elegans' to perfection.

Propagation All the varieties listed here are normally increased from 3–4in (8–10cm) tip cuttings taken in spring or autumn. Use rooting preparation and root in warmth at 60°F (16°C). Pot up singly when rooted and grow on for two to four years before planting out.

Problems Unlikely.

Cryptomeria Japonica 'Elegans'

Japanese Cedar
Hardiness HR3
Evergreen conifer

Description A very desirable small tree of broadly columnar habit; ht 15ft (4.5m), reaching 10ft (3m) in about ten years. The main attraction is the soft, feathery foliage which alternates from delicate bronze-green in summer to coppery-red in autumn and winter.

Varieties There are plenty of garden-worthy varieties, noted for their foliage and form. Only a short selection can be mentioned here (sizes indicated are average at ten years after planting). *C.j.* 'Elegans Compacta'; ht 5ft (1.5m) – bushy, dense oval habit; soft browny-green summer foliage turns to purple in winter. *C.j.* 'Elegans Nana'; ht 20in (50cm) – dense, rounded habit with bronze winter foliage. *C.j.* 'Sekkan Sugi'; ht 7ft (2m) – conical outline with striking creamy summer foliage, turning bronze in winter. Somewhat frost and wind sensitive. *C.j.* 'Vilmoriniana'; ht 12in (30cm) – rounded, compact and bushy, green summer foliage turns purple in winter.

Position and use Japanese cedars grow well in light partial shade – but nothing too dark or foliage colouring will be pale. A sheltered garden is needed. A sunny west-facing position is the best – provided it is sheltered from midday sun.

A moist but free-draining, fertile, lime-free medium loam – well supplied with peat or leaf mould – is the ideal.

Given shade, shelter and moisture, Japanese cedars are excellent for rock gardens, waterside and as single specimens or groupings in grass and mixed plantings. One of the best for containers.

Treatment   Seek out container-raised stock of not more than 20in (50cm) in height. Plant out during mild weather in April and May. Use anti-wilt preparation at planting time. Give protection from frost and shelter from wind for the first few winters. This is vital with container grown trees which need special care and root protection during a hard winter. Japanese Cedars must be kept moist at all times until well established. Pruning is minimal apart from shaping when necessary – in late spring/early summer. Correct any tendency to fork. See *Abies koreana*, page 116.

Propagation   The Japanese cedar varieties mentioned above do not come true from seed. So take 4in (10cm) semi-ripewood cuttings in August and September. Root in warmth at 60–65°F (16–18°C). Pot up singly and grow on for two to four years.

Problems   The chief hazards are frost, wind and dryness.

× *Cupressocyparis Leylandii* 'Castlewellan'

Golden Leyland Cypress
Hardiness HRI
Evergreen conifer

Description   A quick-growing, medium to large-sized, broadly columnar tree; ht to 40ft (12m) and more, growing as much as 3½ft (1m) per annum. The foliage is coarsely feather, golden in summer becoming golden-bronze in winter. Seed is rarely produced – but when it is, is carried in small round cones.

Varieties   The following varieties are all broadly similar to the golden Leyland cypress as regards size, shape, growth rate and foliage form. *C.l.*

Fig 94   The gold and green × cupressocyparis leylandii 'Castlewellan' is quick growing, good for instant effects, but ultimately grows too large for small gardens.

'Argentea Variegata' – green foliage is spotted and blotched with white. *C.l.* 'Haggerstone Grey' – an old variety, which is coming increasingly scarce, but worth seeking out if grey-green foliage effects appeal. *C.l.* 'Robinson's Gold' – its bright yellow summer foliage turns to golden-bronze in winter. *C.l.notabilis* forms a dark grey-green columnar tree.

Position and use   All the varieties mentioned grow well in sun or partial shade. They are not too fussy about shelter. Leyland cypress stand up to wind and, even if scorched, will quickly outgrow all but the most severe disfigurements.

Any reasonably fertile, free-draining garden soil will do – including chalky.

Leyland cypress are excellent for use as quick-growing screens and windbreaks. They stand up to coastal winds and even some sea spray. Use as specimens and in groupings. Try two or three varieties in a group of contrasting colours – say, gold with green and grey.

Treatment Using container-raised trees, preferably not more than 2ft (60cm) in height, plant out in autumn or spring. In windy gardens use anti-wilt preparation at planting time – and stake and tie securely. Often marketed bare root in prepacks – be wary, success rates are low, and they will need nursing along. To thicken up screens, lightly clip in the sides once or twice during summer. Cut back any scorched tips at the same time. Correct any tendency to forking – see *Abies koreana*.

Propagation Take 4in (10cm) semi-ripewood cuttings in September. Root in containers indoors at 60°F (16°C). Pot up singly in spring when well rooted and grow on for one or two years.

Problems Unlikely.

Ginkgo Biloba

Maidenhair Tree
Hardiness HR2
Deciduous conifer

Description A somewhat unusual small to medium-sized tree; ht to about 25ft (7.5m). The habit is columnar or narrowly pyramidal in the early years – then the growth rate quickens. The foliage differs from other conifers. The flat fan-shaped leaves resemble the leaflets of a maidenhair fern. Hence the name. The yellow-green summer foliage turns a soft golden yellow in autumn before leaf fall. Also, unlike most other conifers, trees are either male or female. But for practical purposes this is academic since flowering and fruiting are rare.

Varieties The following garden-worthy forms grow to 20–23ft (6–7m) – reaching about 10ft (3m) in ten years. *G.b.* 'Fastigiata' – columnar with sharply ascending branches and foliage similar to *G.biloba*. *G.b.* 'Tremonia' – similar to *G.b.* 'Fastigiata', but with a narrowly conical habit. *G.b.* 'Variegata' – similar to *G.biloba*, but smaller in size and the green leaves are banded with creamy-white variegation.

Position and use The maidenhair tree does best in a warm, sunny situation, but it will stand partial shade without ill effect. An open, yet sheltered site is preferred. But the tree will adapt

Fig 95 Ginkgo biloba, *the Maidenhair Tree, is slow growing but ultimately makes a sizeable tree. It has golden autumn leaf tints.*

to a fair amount of wind and cold. It is hardier than it looks.

A good average garden soil that is free draining and fertile is adequate. Tolerant of some chalk content.

The maidenhair tree makes a useful specimen in grass or hardstanding area. A curiosity tree for the shrub border. Does well in containers.

Treatment Buy small container-raised stock of no more than 2ft (60cm) in height. Plant out in April or May during mild, showery weather. The maidenhair tree suffers if it is allowed to go short of water if the atmosphere is too dry. So keep moist and mulch generously until well established. Pruning needs should be minimal – only sufficient to keep trees iin shape – and confined to autumn.

Propagation The above named varieties are grafted on to seedling rootstocks in March – indoors. Grow on for three to four years before planting out, giving frame protection for the first two years.

Raising *Ginkgo biloba* from imported seed is quite commonplace. Sow in October in containers under a frame to chill. Move into warmth in late winter. Germinate at 60–65°F (16–18°C). Pot up singly and grow on for about four years before 'working' or planting out.

Problems Nothing serious as a rule.

Juniperus Communis 'Suecica'

Juniper
Hardiness HRI
Evergreen conifer

Description Normally makes a slow-growing small tree conifer, ht about 7ft (2m) ten years after planting. But is capable of ultimately reaching 25ft (7.5m) and more. Narrow pyramidal in habit with basal branching – and foliage retained well near to ground level. The aromatic, prickly foliage is blue-green all year round. Mature junipers carry round pea-sized green berries – which turn violet or purple on ripening.

Varieties All sizes quoted refer to ten years from planting. *J.chinensis* 'Aurea'; ht 7ft (2m), of pyramidal outline with gold and green foliage. *J.c.* 'Pyramidalis'; ht 6–7ft (1.8–2m), pyramidal with grey or steely blue foliage. *J.communis* 'Compressa Compacta'; ht 2ft (60cm), columnar and compact with blue-green foliage. *J.communis* 'Hibernica', Irish juniper; ht to 6–7ft (1.8–2m), makes an attractive blue-green column of foliage. *J.scopulorum*; ht 7–8ft (2–2.4m), pyramidal in habit, quick-growing with silver-blue foliage. *J.virginiana* 'Skyrocket'; ht 7–9ft (2–2.7m), a quick-growing pyramidal pencil cedar with grey-blue summer foliage becoming grey in winter.

Position and use Junipers do best in warm, sunny sites. But partial shade is no serious handicap. These are very hardy trees which can tolerate exposed windswept sites – where growth is obviously going to be slower than in favoured, sheltered situations. A good tree for the coast.

Any reasonable, fertile, well-drained garden soil that is neutral to chalk, rather than acid, will do. Thin shallow soils are tolerated.

Use As specimen trees in lawns and hardstanding areas, in rock gardens, near doorways, in raised beds and in containers.

Treatment Carry out all planting during April and May – in the ground and in containers. Set out small stock – no more than ht 2–3ft (60–90cm). Protect from cold wind during the first winter after planting. Little pruning is necessary other than shortening straggly growths – sometime between late May and August.

Propagation Take 3–4in (8–10cm) semi-ripe-wood cuttings in September. Root in containers under a cold frame. Pot up singly when rooted and grow on for three to four years.

Problems Nothing serious is likely.

Picea Glauca 'Albertiana Conica'

Spruce
Hardiness HR2
Evergreen conifer

Description A highly valued dwarf tree; ht to about 4ft (l.2m) ten years after planting. Is of a naturally neat and perfectly conical habit. The dense textured foliage is made up of bright green needles and almost luminous shoot tips – outstanding in spring. The branches break away from the base, just above ground level, and retain their foliage well, covering up any tendency to bare stems. The foliage is aromatic, giving off a distinct, pleasing, clean scent during hot weather.

Varieties The following is but a short choice selection from among the many garden-worthy spruces. Sizes are at ten years from planting. *P.omorika* 'Nana'; ht to 3½ft (lm), forms a compact slow-growing pyramid of light green. *P.pungens glauca* 'Koster', Koster's Blue Spruce; ht to 8ft (2.4m), an outstanding conical tree with vivid silver-blue year-round foliage. *P.p.* 'Globosa'; ht to 2ft (60cm), a dwarf compact, broadly conical blue spruce with bright blue-grey foliage.

Position and use Most spruce grow well in both sun and partial shade. But the blue varieties colour up best in full sun. A sheltered site is preferred and will ensure improved growth.

A deep moisture-retentive, yet well-drained fertile soil which is lime free is required to avoid disappointments.

Spruce make excellent focal points when used in the rock garden, beside the pool and in raised beds. They excel when planted with heathers and dwarf rhododendrons. Useful in containers.

Treatment Generally speaking, all planting into the ground and into containers is best completed during autumn. But delay until spring in cold gardens or where the soil is heavy. Use container-raised young trees, preferably no more than ht 12in (30cm). Use an anti-wilt proprietary preparation at planting time. Protect young trees from wind during the first winter after planting. Minimal pruning is called for.

Propagation Graft all the varieties listed indoors – during March or April on to seedling rootstocks. Use *P.glauca* for *P.g.* 'Albertiana Conica'; *P.omorika* for *P.o.* 'Nana'; and *P.pungens* for *P.p. glauca* 'Koster' and *P.p.* 'Globosa'. Grow on with frame protection for two years. Then for a further two years outdoors – but continue to give winter cover.

To raise rootstocks, sow in November and chill under a frame for eight weeks. Move into warmth at 60°F (16°C). Pot up singly and grow on as for grafted trees.

Problems Nothing serious as a rule.

Pinus Mugo

Mountain Pine
Hardiness HRI
Evergreen conifer

Description A dwarf or small tree of variable height – from about 3½–10ft (1–3m). Usually rounded or spreading and bushy in habit – with characteristic basal branching near soil level. The leaves are typical of pine – long, slender, needle-like and dark green. In spring, attractive pale green new needles are carried at the tips of branches on light brown candle-like shoots.

Varieties The size, colouring and shape of the following selected varieties are less variable than *P.mugo* and, in fact, they are more widely grown. Most will eventually reach 3–5ft (1–1.5m). (Sizes quoted are the average for ten years after planting.) *P.m.* 'Humpy'; ht about 16in (40cm) – rounded habit with mid-green needles. *P.m.* 'Mops'; ht to 2ft (60cm) – rounded habit with grey-green foliage. *P.m.* 'Ophir'; ht to 16in (40cm) – rounded or dome-shaped with beautiful gold-tipped needles. *P.sylvestris* 'Beauvronensis', makes an attractive rounded or pyramidal

Fig 96 Pinus mugo, *the mountain pine, is somewhat variable in habit, ranging from prostrate ground-hugging forms to upright small trees as here.*

mound of grey-green needles – growing to 2½ft (75cm) in height. *P.s.* 'Hibernica'; ht to 2ft (60cm) – round or conical outline. First class with bright grey-blue needles.

Position and use Mountain pines grow best in full sun and open, airy situations. However, the green foliage forms will stand partial shade. Being compact and very hardy, these trees will stand up to considerable exposure.

Any free-draining garden soil of average fertility will suffice. Although acid soils are preferred, those with modest chalk content are tolerated.

Planted singly or in groups, pines are excellent in rock gardens, on banks and in containers. They do well in raised beds and are well suited to mixed conifer plantings.

Treatment Seek out small container-raised stock – of not more than 12–16in (30–40cm) high. This is to reduce root disturbance to a minimum. Otherwise risk a setback. Carry out all planting during autumn or spring. Protect from wind during the first winter – until established. Pruning is not normally needed or desirable – apart from cutting out dead or damaged branches in late spring.

Propagation Graft all the varieties mentioned in March – on to seed-raised *P.mugo* rootstocks. Grow under frames for two years after grafting. Then move outdoors for a further two years, making sure they have winter protection, before planting out.

To raise rootstocks, sow *P.mugo* in summer or autumn under frames. Prick out singly into pots and grow on for two years under frames. Then for a further two years in the open before 'working'.

Problems Unlikely.

Taxus Baccata 'Standishii'

Yew
Hardiness HRI
Evergreen conifer

Description A small long-lived, slow-growing tree; ht eventually 12–15ft (3.5–4.5m). Expect it to reach a height of 7ft (2m) ten years after planting out. Normally makes a multi-stemmed tree of narrow columnar habit, sporting attractive green and gold variegated needle-type foliage to give year-round interest.

Varieties *Taxus baccata*. Common yew; ht 8ft (2.5m) at ten years and ultimately a small to medium-sized spreading tree up to 35ft (10–15m) or more. Male and female flowers are formed on separate trees with female trees producing the familiar red autumn berries. The foliage is dark green. Often grown as a single-stemmed tree as well as the popular multi-stemmed specimens.

Fig 97   The golden Irish yew, Taxus baccata 'Fastigiata Aureomarginata' tolerates dry conditions and alkaline soils better than most conifers.

T.b. 'Aurea'; ht about 5ft (1.5m) after ten years – a golden, slower-growing, smaller form of *T. baccata* with spreading habit. *T.b.* 'Fastigiata', the Irish yew; ht to 6ft (1.8m) after ten years – forms a narrow upright column, with dark green foliage. *T.b.* 'Fastigiata Aureomarginata'; ht to 5ft (1.5m) after ten years, a golden Irish yew.

Position and use   Yews are suitable for most situations. All do well in sun and partial shade. But those with golden foliage are less well adapted than the green-leaved kinds to permanent sunless sites where they are likely to lose their golden colouring. In all but the most exposed gardens they are tolerant of moderate wind.

Any reasonable free-draining, average garden soil – including chalky – will suffice. But don't plant yews in shallow gravelly soils, liable to dry out badly in hot weather.

Yews are most adaptable. Use them as specimens in grass and hard-surfaced areas, in pairs to frame views, as focal points in mixed plantings, as topiary for screening and in containers.

NOTE: Don't plant yews within reach of grazing animals in view of the poisonous nature of the foliage and seeds.

Treatment   Carry out all planting – in the ground and containers – during autumn and spring. Choose young container-grown stock of preferably no more than 20in (50cm) in height. Protect from wind during the first winter after planting. Little or no pruning is needed apart perhaps from clipping to shape and removing damaged branches – work best carried out between late spring and late summer. Topiary needs regular clipping – three or four times during the growing season. If multi-stem trees look like getting out of shape, encircle inconspicuously with wire before the onset of winter.

Propagation   Take 4in (10cm) semi-ripe cuttings in September/early October and root under a cold frame. Pot up when rooted and grow on for two to three years. Give frost protection each winter while in containers.

Problems   Nothing serious as a rule.

Thuja Occidentalis 'Rheingold'

Arborvitae
Hardiness HR2
Evergreen conifer

Description A popular, dwarf tree with a broadly conical habit; ht to 5ft (1.5m). The ultimate height is achieved in about ten years and then the tree spreads outwards. The faintly aromatic gold and amber foliage, which retains its colour year round, is the main attraction. It is feathery, fairly dense and carried from almost ground level upwards.

Varieties The following are well-tried, choice garden varieties which have aromatic foliage – but a short selection from among many. The sizes quoted are as at ten years after planting. *T.occidentalis* 'Danica'; ht about 16in (40cm), dwarf globose habit and dense green summer foliage, changing to bronze in winter. *T.o.* 'Golden Globe'; ht to 2ft (60cm), dwarf, rounded habit with golden-yellow year-round foliage. *T.o.* 'Holmstrup'; ht to 8ft (2.4m), a densely textured

Fig 98 The delightful coppery-golden Thuja occidentalis 'Rheingold' is a useful addition to any garden, large or small.

dwarf tree conifer of slender conical habit. Foliage remains dark green year round. *T.o.* 'Smaragd'; ht to 10ft (3m), forms a narrow column of deep green; colour retained throughout the year.

Position and use Sun or partial shade will suit most varieties. But those with gold foliage colour up best in sun. These gold varieties also benefit from careful siting. Choose sheltered situations, out of the direct path of cold and drying north and east winds. The green foliage varieties will tolerate exposed gardens within limits.

Any reasonably fertile, deep garden soil that is free draining and high in organic matter, should suffice. Thujas are tolerant of drier and chalkier conditions than many other conifers.

All Thujas make useful focal points – as single specimens and in groups. The tall green-foliaged varieties are useful for screening. The dwarf kinds are excellent for rock gardens, planting with heathers, for use in raised beds, containers and sink gardens.

Treatment Plant out container-raised, small stock, preferably no more than ht 2ft (60cm) during spring – both when planting into the ground and into containers. Alternatively, given a mild climate, and a sheltered, warm garden, plant out in autumn. Protect young Thuja from wind and frost during the first winter or two after planting. Little pruning is needed apart from cutting out deadwood and scorched foliage – work best carried out in late spring.

Propagation Take 3–4in (8–10cm) semi-ripe wood cuttings in September/October from all the varieties mentioned. Root under a cold frame, or in a greenhouse. Pot up singly when rooted and grow on for two or three years overwintering under cover.

Problems Thuja blight can attack. Cut out badly affected, blackened, dying foliage in the early stages. Spray with fungicide right away. Otherwise fairly trouble free.

127

Index